# a BRIDGE to inspired declarer play

Julian Laderman Author of *A Bridge to Simple Squeezes*

MASTER POINT PRESS
TORONTO • CANADA

4115706

Master Point Press
331 Douglas Ave.
Toronto, Ontario, Canada
M5M 1H2      (416)781-0351
Email:      info@masterpointpress.com
Websites:   www.masterpointpress.com
            www.masteringbridge.com
            www.bridgeblogging.com
            www.ebooksbridge.com


**Library and Archives Canada Cataloguing in Publication**

Laderman, Julian

    A bridge to inspired declarer play / written by Julian Laderman.

Includes index.

ISBN 978-1-897106-44-0

    1. Contract bridge.  I. Title.

GV1282.3.L25 2009            795.41'53        C2008-907543-9

Editor                          Ray Lee
Copy editor/interior format     Sally Sparrow
Cover and interior design       Olena S. Sullivan/New Mediatrix

1 2 3 4 5 6 7        13 12 11 10 09

*In memory of my parents,*
*Marion and Jack Laderman*

# ACKNOWLEDGMENTS

I want to thank many individuals who were helpful in creating this book.

My bridge partners Howard Marks and Ivan Petrovic were my 'two right arms' during the writing process. They suggested many important changes and ideas that improved the approach and content of *A Bridge to Inspired Declarer Play*.

The following bridge partners and friends helped by either providing me with useful input on the individual problems or the final manuscript: Mohan Dutt, Dennis Kaye, Sandy Prosnitz, Art Seelenfreund, Barbara Skluth, and Stuart Weinberg. Alex Alberts did the photo.

I am extremely grateful to Amalia Ottemberg who suggested many improvements in style and phrasing that helped clarify the presentation.

I want to thank Antoinette Blum, a non-bridge player, but my partner in life for her patience and support. Since she has never played a single hand of bridge, she always feels that my hand analysis is brilliant. A wonderful system of reinforcement!

I am also grateful to Linda and Ray Lee of Master Point Press for suggesting numerous ways to improve the book and for an excellent job of editing the manuscript. I would also like to thank Sally Sparrow for her great copyediting and layout.

# TABLE OF CONTENTS

# INTRODUCTION

## *What is 'inspired' declarer play?*

Readers of my column in *The Bronx Journal* have often told me that they enjoyed and understood the columns but regretted that in the heat of battle they would not be able to execute the key play. Actually they usually confess that they would not even consider the winning line. This comment certainly points to one of the greatest challenges facing bridge players. When the dummy hits the table, declarer will usually take less than a minute to make a decision on how to approach a hand: endplay, crossruff, suit establishment, etc. The title *A Bridge to Inspired Declarer Play* was chosen to indicate that this book tries to attack the problem head-on. The goal is to enable declarer to identify those features of a hand which should inspire him to consider and select the correct line of play.

In a typical textbook on declarer play the reader studies examples and does exercises. Since each chapter usually covers a different type of play, the reader has a wonderful clue on how to approach any hand in the book by merely looking at the name of the chapter. A bridge book of this sort is fine for learning the technique of executing a play, but does little to train a declarer to consider that line of play at the table. Since bridge columns in newspapers or books are not categorized, these hands don't usually 'give away the ending' to the reader before he reads the column.

A few books have tried to develop a declarer's intuition on how to approach a hand. An excellent book that focuses attention on this problem is Freddie North's *Bridge Play Unraveled*.[1] The author begins with a useful 40-page glossary of techniques and then the reader is tested with 58 problems. Guy Levé's recent book *The Encyclopedia of Card Play Techniques at Bridge*[2] does an excellent job of classifying declarer play techniques and providing numerous examples. In my previous book, *A Bridge to Simple Squeezes*[3], the first chapter is

---

1. Freddie North, *Bridge Play Unraveled. Recognition is Everything* (London: Batsford, 2003).
2. Guy Levé, *The Encyclopedia of Card Play Techniques at Bridge* (Toronto: Master Point Press, 2007).
3. Julian Laderman, *A Bridge to Simple Squeezes*, 2nd ed. (Toronto: Master Point Press, 2007).

entirely devoted to developing recognition of the characteristics of a hand that should inspire a declarer to look for a squeeze. Those features will not mean that a squeeze play can be executed, but will merely trigger the declarer to be on the alert and consider squeeze possibilities. A player cannot recognize the correct line of play if he does not consider that line of play.

A Bridge to Inspired Declarer Play consists of 38 problems that are not organized by type of play.[4] At the end of each problem there is a section that provides information on what features of a hand should inspire declarer to consider the correct line of play.

## Correct plays that violate bridge instincts

When I created these deals my goal was to demonstrate principles that were not only useful and simple, but also easily overlooked. A play is easily overlooked if it goes against a bridge player's instinct – for example, winning a trick with a higher card than necessary. We will see deals where declarer plays an unnecessarily high card, possibly to create an entry. An analogous play is when declarer discards a winner and keeps a loser.

Losing tricks also goes against a bridge player's instinct. Since the goal is to win tricks, it is easy for declarer to overlook crucial situations where the winning line involves losing a trick or tricks. One must always remember that the real goal is to win as many of the thirteen tricks as possible. Declarers must think beyond winning the present trick. A relevant expression is 'We won the battle but lost the war'. A common theme of many of the problems in this book is that declarer has to lose a trick that could be won. A variation of this is not losing a trick on purpose, but rather not trying to win one. If your curiosity cannot be contained, go straight to Problem 1. In my usual heavy-handed style, at the end of each problem I comment on whether the correct play involved intentionally losing a trick or not trying to win a trick. While reading this book, one should be on the alert for this technique.

Another theme recurring in the problems is that declarers often concentrate too much on their own hand and not enough on dummy.

---

4. The deals have appeared with shorter explanations in a newspaper column in *The Bronx Journal*.

It is often easier to count losers in dummy than in declarer's hand. This is particularly true when the trump suit is longer in dummy's hand than in declarer's, such as after a transfer bid. This mistake is partially induced by declarer being focused on his own hand for several minutes prior to dummy making an appearance on the table.

The last but most important theme is that many mistakes occur on the first trick. When dummy hits the table one must plan the hand and carry out many activities: counting winners, counting losers, absorbing any bidding by the defense and digesting the opening lead. In a duplicate event, declarer must even consider alternative contracts that other pairs may be in, both playing in the same direction and in the other direction. Stage magicians know that the key to success is to divert their victim's attention. Unfortunately, so do pickpockets! Declarer, too, can easily fall victim to a diversion. When dummy appears there is so much new information for declarer to absorb, it is easy to forget the bidding or fail to draw all the possible inferences from the opening lead. Declarer should try to get into the habit of concentrating on the defenders' bids while the defense is deciding on the opening lead. Sometimes when I am declarer and dummy has a singleton in the suit of the opening lead, my partner may try to be helpful and push the singleton a few inches to indicate that it is being played. I tell my partner to return the singleton since I want to admire my full dummy. Most of the problems in this book require declarer to avoid a mistake on the first or second trick.

Virtually all books on declarer play, as well as books on common mistakes, tell readers to take their time and plan the whole hand before playing from dummy on the first trick. Beginner/intermediate players mistakenly believe, however, that if they take their time on the first trick, they are revealing that they don't know what to do. They fear that they are demonstrating their inexperience and lack of ability. Quite the opposite is true. Bridge is a challenging game. A good player will not rush and skip any of the activities mentioned in the previous paragraph. At duplicate events a bridge player often faces players with whom he is unfamiliar. It is essential for a defender to try to assess the ability of a declarer. This will enable the defender to draw inferences about declarer's ability to choose the proper line of play. For every minute I must wait as a defender on Trick 1, I assume that declarer has 2000 more masterpoints. The more I wait, the more I am impressed by declarer! Of course, after four minutes, when dummy tells declarer to call a card from dummy and declarer slaps himself on the head, declarer immediately loses 8000 masterpoints. I now realize that declarer was perhaps concentrating on whether there was any egg salad left in the food area!

After the first trick declarer should not take too long on other tricks unless something unusual happens in the play. For example, suppose you are in a 4-4 trump fit and the first round of trumps reveals a 5-0 break. This surprise should cause you to re-examine your whole line of play. Faced with this turn of events, you may decide to drop your original plan of perhaps establishing a long side suit in dummy in favor of a crossruff.

All too often bridge players react to a 5-0 break like a boxer who has just been hit by a very hard punch. Boxers shake their heads to indicate that they are not hurt and rush toward their opponents as proof. This macho approach is not good for either a boxer or a bridge player.

## Slow losers are inspirational

It is important to distinguish between two different types of losers. Consider these alternatives for a side suit in a trump contract.

**Case 1:** Dummy has xxx and declarer has AKx

**Case 2:** Dummy has xxx and declarer has KQJ.

In both cases, declarer expects to win two tricks and lose one. That is where the similarity ends. In the first case declarer has a third-round loser. This gives declarer time to use another suit to discard that one loser. Declarer even has time to lose tricks while setting up a winner in another suit for a discard from this suit.

In Case 2, declarer has a first-round loser. Declarer would need three discards from another suit to avoid that loser. Declarer cannot lose any tricks in the process, since the loser in Case 2 can immediately be grabbed by the defense.

It is useful to label a loser as either a **fast loser** or a **slow loser**. Obviously, Case 1 demonstrates a slow loser and Case 2 a fast loser. Many examples in this book involve disposing of slow losers. When planning the play of a hand, slow losers should inspire declarer to search the other side suits for possible ways to discard those losers. Clearly declarer must focus on all four suits rather than just the suit of the present trick.

A **mirror distribution** refers to the situation when declarer and dummy have the same length in all four suits. These hands can have a wealth of high card points but still limited trick-winning ability since no suit can provide discards of slow losers in another suit.

## Exercises for generalizing the type of play

Sometimes I get flashbacks to my childhood, when my parents would take me to a diner. It was not uncommon to be seated in front of a place mat with a complicated pattern, my parents pulling out a pencil and encouraging me to find the 12 elephants hidden in the intricacies. I now realize that the purpose was less for my entertainment than to keep me busy and give my parents freedom to chat without my butting in. I suppose the place mat designer first drew the 12 elephants and then drew the rest of the pattern to hide them. It is never easy to hide an elephant. This is not unlike the process of creating a bridge column. One starts with a type of play, then lays out the cards needed for that play, and finally fills in the rest of the deal. In many ways this chore of creating deals is easier than that of playing our difficult game. One does not have to be triggered into recognizing the type of play since one starts out choosing a type of play. After deciding on a play, the process of choosing the right cards to demonstrate it can involve difficult decisions. There are always many desirable alternatives.

Readers should appreciate that even though a play technique in this book is illustrated by a specific deal, it is necessary to be able to recognize a broader class of hands where the same type of play could be applied. This is necessary if you are going to be able to find the play at the bridge table. I have therefore included an unusual set of exercises in an attempt to develop a reader's ability to generalize a play. After each problem, I ask the reader to modify the deal slightly to create a new example of the same type of play. There are many possible correct answers to every exercise, but in Section 2, pages 117-136, I provide a sample answer for each one.

I have some misgivings about these exercises. Sometimes the answers are rather obvious. As a teacher, I prefer the type of exercises for which there is only one correct answer. So just think of these exercises as an alternative example demonstrating the principle in the problem. With luck, you will find them useful for generalizing a principle and feel that they are a valuable learning experience. Either way, if you do run into me at a tournament please let me know if you found these exercises worthwhile. If you don't like them, I won't be offended.

## Appendices on obtaining probabilities

Often when bridge players first pick up the game they are quickly introduced to a bad habit. They are taught that when you play a suit, after one round is played and everyone follows, four cards have been played in the suit; after two rounds are played and everyone follows, eight cards have been played in the suit. There is nothing incorrect about this statement but, instead, one must learn to think about how the suit can split. For instance, suppose between your hand and dummy you have eight cards in a suit. This leaves the two defenders with five cards and they will split 3-2, 4-1 or 5-0. Now, if both defenders follow for two rounds of that suit, there is only one card remaining in this suit. Thinking in terms of suit splits is much less mentally taxing and is an essential skill for counting a hand.

It is not only important to think of how a suit may split but also the likelihood of each possibility.

| For 2 cards held by the defense | | For 3 cards held by the defense | |
|---|---|---|---|
| 1-1 | 52% | 2-1 | 78% |
| 2-0 | 48% | 3-0 | 22% |

| For 4 cards held by the defense | | For 5 cards held by the defense | |
|---|---|---|---|
| 2-2 | 40% | 3-2 | 68% |
| 3-1 | 50% | 4-1 | 28% |
| 4-0 | 10% | 5-0 | 4% |

| For 6 cards held by the defense | | For 7 cards held by the defense | |
|---|---|---|---|
| 3-3 | 36% | 4-3 | 62% |
| 4-2 | 48% | 5-2 | 31% |
| 5-1 | 15% | 6-1 | 7% |
| 6-0 | 1% | 7-0 | <1% |

Actually if you just commit to memory the first two lines of each of these six cases, you will have virtually all the information you will need at the bridge table. Only these twelve values need to be memorized. Occasionally during a post-mortem, I will mention the likelihood of a particular split and someone will say, 'You know that because you are a mathematician'. They are surprised when I tell them that I had memorized the value. Even though these values are indeed easy to figure out, I'm sure my opponents would object if I took a couple of minutes to scribble on a sheet of paper. I can hear the **DIRECTOR** call!

These tables are most useful when comparing alternative ways to play a hand *prior to playing any tricks*. The percentages are in flux during the play of the hand, as more information becomes available. The auction, too, affects the probabilities. For example, suppose the opponents are willing to sell out to you at a low level while holding almost 20 high card points; the chance of their having voids or singletons is less than the values in these tables.

The above six tables are based on not having any information either about that suit or about how any other suits are split. For example, if you are missing seven cards in a suit and you learn they are split 6-1, the percentages in the tables are no longer valid guides to how any other suit is split. The Appendices explain how to calculate the correct percentages for the other three suits. The technique for obtaining these values is not difficult but they cannot be computed in the middle of a hand. If you are armed with a calculator, the calculations can be done when there is a break between rounds. So the technique is useless to you while playing a hand, but may be invaluable during the post-mortem when you want to convince your partner that you made the proper decision.

This book includes two appendices on probability. *Appendix 1: Everything You Ever Wanted to Know About Probability* starts with the very basics of probability. It includes a section on how to use and misuse the values in the above tables and a section on the play of several suit combinations. In most of the problems there is a passing reference to the likelihood of some event. At the end of Appendix 1, I refer back to all the percentages that appeared throughout the problems and explain how those values were obtained.

Sometimes bridge players will ask me questions about how the values in the tables can be obtained. For the curious reader, *Appendix 2: Much More Than You Ever Wanted to Know About Probability* demonstrates how to calculate them. The reader is first provided with a background in combinatorics.

As stated earlier, the goal of this book is to help declarer find the best line of play on a hand. He must often choose between different alternatives. A knowledge of the basics of probability is necessary for declarer to be able to compare the likelihood of success of each line.

## Presentation

The problems in this book were created primarily to exhibit declarer play and not to teach a bidding system. However the bidding is always provided since the defenders' bids or passes may be the key to some hands. At times I explain some bids that I feel may not be understood by a typical reader. I even take the opportunity to present a few conventions that may be new to some readers. If you purchased this book in the hope it would present a cohesive bidding system, you will be disappointed; but you should have paid attention to the title! Of course, even though this is a book on declarer play, I often make comments about the defense.

This next paragraph is copied verbatim from my book *A Bridge to Simple Squeezes* since it is equally relevant: "While writing this book, I frequently stumbled over which pronoun to use when referring to the declarer. **He/She** is cumbersome, **He** alone seems male chauvinistic, and alternating **he** and **she** is a distraction. When I explained my problem to a female bridge partner, Sandy Prosnitz, her advice was 'When declarer plays correctly use **she**. When declarer makes a mistake use **he**.' Since my declarers are brilliant, that would mean using **she** all the time. I finally decided to use **he**, since it takes less time to type."

Many readers may wish to first consider the play of a hand without the distraction of seeing both the defenders' cards and the explanatory text appearing on the same page. Therefore the 38 deals are presented first as problems before their key points are discussed on the following pages.

At the end of *A Bridge to Inspired Declarer Play* there is an *Index of Types of Plays*. This index enables a reader who wants to see examples of a particular play to go directly to the appropriate problems. Most problems demonstrate more than one type of play.

It's time to get to some bridge. I hope you enjoy the book.

# SECTION 1
## Problems

Dealer: North
East-West vul.

**North**
♠ K 6 3 2
♡ J 10 5
◇ J 8 7
♣ K 5 3

**South**
♠ 9 5
♡ A K Q 9 4
◇ 10 4 3
♣ A 4 2

| West | North | East | South |
|------|-------|------|-------|
|      | pass  | pass | 1♡    |
| dbl  | 2♡    | all pass |   |

West leads the ♠Q. Where will your eighth trick come from?

**PROBLEM 2**  HOW A LOSER GOT LOST

Dealer: West
East-West vul.

**North**
♠ Q 10 9 2
♡ 9 7 6
◇ K 5 4
♣ Q J 3

**South**
♠ A K J 8 7 4
♡ A 5 3
◇ A 8 2
♣ 5

| West | North | East | South |
|------|-------|------|-------|
| pass | pass  | pass | 1♠    |
| pass | 2♠    | pass | 3♠    |
| pass | 4♠    | all pass |   |

West leads the ♣A, then shifts to the ♡Q. How will you reduce four losers to three?

## PROBLEM 3 LOOK BEFORE YOU LEAP

Dealer: West
Neither vul.

**North**
♠ Q J 4
♡ 6 5 3
◇ K Q J 10 3
♣ 7 4

**South**
♠ A 3 2
♡ A K 4
◇ 9 7 4
♣ A K 6 5

| West | North | East | South |
|------|-------|------|-------|
| pass | pass | pass | 1♣ |
| pass | 1◇ | pass | 2NT |
| pass | 3NT | all pass | |

West leads the ♠10. How can you be sure of making your contract?

## PROBLEM 4 HARD WORK PAYS OFF

Dealer: East
Both vul.

**North**
♠ K 4
♡ A K 3
◇ 6 5 4 3 2
♣ A K 4

**South**
♠ A Q J 10 7 6 5 3
♡ 7 6
◇ —
♣ 7 5 2

| West | North | East | South |
|------|-------|------|-------|
| | | pass | 4♠ |
| pass | 5♣ | pass | 5◇ |
| pass | 7♠ | all pass | |

West leads the ♣Q. Twelve tricks are easy – but where will the thirteenth come from?

**North**
♠ K 6 3 2
♡ J 10 5
◇ J 8 7
♣ K 5 3

**West**
♠ Q J 10 8
♡ 8 2
◇ A Q 9
♣ Q J 8 6

*Dealer N*
*EW Vul.*

**East**
♠ A 7 4
♡ 7 6 3
◇ K 6 5 2
♣ 10 9 7

**South**
♠ 9 5
♡ A K Q 9 4
◇ 10 4 3
♣ A 4 2

| West | North | East | South |
|---|---|---|---|
|  | pass | pass | 1♡ |
| dbl | 2♡ | all pass |  |

West leads the ♠Q. Where will your eighth trick come from?

Throughout history, one of the most difficult problems faced by society has been to define the value of having a monarch. This same problem has been faced by bridge players trying to evaluate their hands. The king is the card whose value is the hardest to judge. If the defender sitting behind your king holds the ace, and if you have no cards in the suit to promote, the king may have no more value than a lowly deuce.

On the illustrated deal, North had no problem raising to 2♡ with 8 HCP and three hearts. If West had not doubled, North should respond 1♠ in an attempt to find a 4-4 spade fit. However, here West is likely to hold four spades, so even if North-South can find a 4-4 spade fit, they will probably encounter a bad trump break. North's two kings looked very valuable during the bidding since West doubled and East passed. Therefore, from North's perspective, if the defense holds the ♠A or the ♣A they are probably held by West.

Once declarer sees the dummy and the opening lead he realizes that the ♣K is very useful but the ♠K is poorly placed. At first glance the ♠K appears worthless. Declarer must not play the ♠K in desperation, hoping that West led the ♠Q while holding the ♠A – an overwhelmingly unlikely scenario. Declarer should play the ♠2 from dummy and concede the first trick to West. If West continues with the ♠J, declarer must remain patient and play the ♠3 from dummy. Assume West now shifts to a club. South can win with the ♣A and pull the defenders trumps in three rounds, winning the third round in dummy. Declarer can now play the ♠6 and have the pleasure of trumping East's ace. Eventually declarer can enter dummy with the ♣K and discard a small club on the ♠K.

If West had led spades on the first three rounds, declarer would have had to play a small card from dummy on all three tricks. The third trick would be ruffed by declarer. This would establish the ♠K and the contract would succeed. If the defense had shifted to clubs after the first round of spades, declarer would have had to attack spades before playing three rounds of trumps so as to be able to use the trump suit as an entry to dummy to establish the ♠K.

If the defense had attacked clubs on the opening lead, declarer would not have had the timing to set up the ♠K for a club discard. The contract would have been set since the defense would have taken six tricks: three diamonds, one club, and two spades.

Was declarer very fortunate that West started with four spades and East with three including the ace? Actually this position can be anticipated from the bidding and the opening lead. West might have overcalled 1♠ had he held five or more spades, so declarer should expect West to have at most four spades. Meanwhile, East probably would have bid 2♠ had he held four spades to the ace, so East has at most three. Therefore declarer can expect the seven spades held by the defense to be divided four with West and three with East. If the defense calls declarer lucky, he can point out why he expected the ace to fall on the third round and gain their respect, at least as a bridge player!

Don't let the defense turn your king into a deuce. Fight off an attack on your king.

**Type of play:** Establish a winner in dummy. Card reading.

**Inspirational features:**
1)  The ♠K is almost certainly sitting helplessly under a defender's ace.
2)  More length in dummy's spade suit than the defender with the ace.
3)  No potential for promoting a lower-ranking card in the spade suit.
4)  A slow loser in the club suit. (This play would fail if declarer held a fast loser in clubs.)

**Lose trick or do not try to win a trick:** Don't try to win a trick with the king until it is a winner.

**Create deal exercise:** Modify this deal so that dummy has the ♠Q instead of the ♠K, but the same technique works.

**North**
- ♠ Q 10 9 2
- ♡ 9 7 6
- ◇ K 5 4
- ♣ Q J 3

**West**
- ♠ 6 3
- ♡ Q J 4
- ◇ 10 9 6 3
- ♣ A K 9 7

*Dealer W*
*EW Vul.*

**East**
- ♠ 5
- ♡ K 10 8 2
- ◇ Q J 7
- ♣ 10 8 6 4 2

**South**
- ♠ A K J 8 7 4
- ♡ A 5 3
- ◇ A 8 2
- ♣ 5

| West | North | East | South |
|------|-------|------|-------|
| pass | pass | pass | 1♠ |
| pass | 2♠ | pass | 3♠ |
| pass | 4♠ | all pass | |

West leads the ♣A, then shifts to the ♡Q. How will you reduce four losers to three?

When a bridge player has to make an opening lead he is elated to find a suit in which he holds both the ace and the king. Leading either the ace or king of that suit is considered one of the most desirable leads. It will rarely hurt the defense. However, even though all bridge books endorse leading the suit, there are differing opinions as whether to lead the ace or the king. The standard lead from this holding is still considered by some to be the king, but most modern bridge partnerships have switched over to leading the ace. The difficulty with leading the king from this holding is that the king would also be led if the opening leader holds both the king and the queen but not the ace. Therefore, in some cases when the king is led, the partner of the opening leader may not be able to tell which holding is held by the leader. The difficulty with leading the ace is that there are occasions when the opening leader leads the ace even though he does not have the king. When this occurs, the partner of the opening leader may be misled as to who holds the king. A third alternative is for a partnership to have the understanding that the lead of an ace requires partner to respond with an attitude signal, while the king asks for count.

In this problem, the ace was led from the A-K combination. The deal is an example of a rare situation where this lead was unfortunate for the defense. Of course, whatever is unfortunate for the defense is fortunate for the declarer. Declarer is looking at four losers: one club, one diamond and two hearts. Suppose the defense shifts to a heart after winning the club ace. This will convert the heart slow losers into fast losers. Declarer can win the heart, play two rounds of spades ending in dummy and play the ♣Q. Even though it is reasonably clear from the opening lead that West holds the ♣K, declarer should not ruff but, instead, discard the ♡3. Eventually declarer will get to dummy and play the ♣J, discarding the ◇2. He will not lose any diamonds, and the 4♠ contract will succeed.

When a losing card is played from both declarer and dummy in different suits (in this case dummy's ♣Q and declarer's ♡3) it is called a *loser-on-loser* play. On this trick a heart loser was converted into a club loser. No obvious gain. An indirect gain is obtained by promoting a club winner, the jack, on which to throw the diamond loser.

If the opening leader had chosen to lead the ♡Q instead of ♣A, this loser-on-loser play would not have been possible since when declarer loses the first round of clubs the defense can immediately grab two heart tricks. In principle, the actual lead is normally a desirable and safe lead so the defense should not be too frustrated that it turned out so badly. The defenders will probably be busy discussing how one of declarer's losers disappeared.

Several problems in this book involve a loser-on-loser play. You will see this play save a trick for many completely different reasons. It is a very versatile play. The fun is to recognize and execute it. Don't be a loser by missing a loser-on-loser play.

**Type of play:** Loser-on-loser. Establish a winner in dummy.

### Inspirational features:
1) Slow loser in the diamond suit. Play would achieve nothing if the loser were a fast loser.
2) The uneven length between declarer and dummy in the club suit.
3) The power of the touching honors in the club suit.

**Lose trick or do not try to win a trick:** Lose a club trick that need not be lost. This play trades a heart loser for a club loser. The advantage is that the other club honor is promoted to a winner.

It is important to observe that declarer must first discard a heart and then the diamond because reversing the order will not work.

**Create deal exercise:** Modify this deal so that declarer must discard two cards in the same suit, rather than in different suits.

**North**
- ♠ Q J 4
- ♡ 6 5 3
- ♢ K Q J 10 3
- ♣ 7 4

**West**
- ♠ 10 9 8 6
- ♡ Q J 7
- ♢ 8 2
- ♣ Q 8 3 2

*Dealer W*
*Neither Vul.*

**East**
- ♠ K 7 5
- ♡ 10 9 8 2
- ♢ A 6 5
- ♣ J 10 9

**South**
- ♠ A 3 2
- ♡ A K 4
- ♢ 9 7 4
- ♣ A K 6 5

| West | North | East | South |
|------|-------|------|-------|
| pass | pass | pass | 1♣ |
| pass | 1♢ | pass | 2NT |
| pass | 3NT | all pass | |

West leads the ♠10. How can you be sure of making your contract?

The lead of the ♠10 allowed declarer to take a 'free finesse' (a finesse without the risk of losing a trick) on the first trick. The ♠J won the first trick when East correctly played low -- a very good play by East that doomed the 3NT contract. When declarer attacked diamonds, East held up his ace until the third round. Since the defense could prevent declarer from getting to dummy with the ♠Q, South ended up winning only eight tricks, two tricks in each suit.

Declarer made the fatal mistake on the first trick. Rather than taking the free finesse, declarer should play the ♠4 from dummy and win the first trick with the ace. Now, after driving out the ♢A, declarer has a guaranteed spade entry to dummy no matter which defender has the ♠K as the ♠Q and ♠J are still both in dummy. This line of play will result in ten tricks since declarer cannot be prevented from taking four diamond tricks. The play of the ♠4 from dummy on the first trick is necessary when the defender with the ♢A has three or more diamonds. If the ♢A is held singleton or doubleton by either defender, it is impossible to hold up until the third round. In this situation declarer can win ten tricks even if he makes the wrong play at the first trick.

Even if West had held the ♠K it would still have been necessary for declarer to win the first trick with the ace in order to ensure an entry. Playing a spade honor from dummy at Trick 1 would win that trick, but there would be no further dummy entries in the spade suit.

West should help out East by signaling properly in the diamond suit. When South wins the second trick with the ◊9 and plays the ◊4 to the third trick, West should play on those two tricks the ◊8 and then the ◊2. This is called a **high low signal** (also known as an 'echo' or 'peter') which tells East that West started with an even number of diamonds. Therefore East will know that declarer started with three diamonds and that it is necessary to hold up until the third round.

Even though free finesses are hard to resist, they often gain nothing. On this hand, after the spade lead, irrespective of where the king is located, declarer will always win exactly two spade tricks. Declarer must not weaken the spade honors in dummy.

South probably made his error before he adjusted his seat and got comfortable as declarer. It is essential to get into the habit of studying dummy and planning the play for the whole hand, not just the suit led, before playing a card from dummy.

Even though that finesse on the first trick is called a free finesse, declarer paid a heavy price for being enticed into it.

**Type of play:** Entry management.

**Inspirational features:**
1) The long diamond suit in dummy.
2) Only two honors in dummy outside of the diamond suit have the potential to serve as an entry. Must not use either before needed.
3) The spade ace may interfere with communication.

**Lose trick or do not try to win a trick:** Don't try to win the first trick with a spade honor in dummy. Surprisingly, it is better to win with the ace than the jack.

**Create deal exercise:** Modify this deal so that declarer can win the first trick in hand with a smaller card than the ace but should still win it with the ace.

**North**
- ♠ K 4
- ♡ A K 3
- ◇ 6 5 4 3 2
- ♣ A K 4

**West**
- ♠ 9
- ♡ Q 10 8 4
- ◇ K J 10 9
- ♣ Q J 10 6

*Dealer E*
*Both Vul.*

**East**
- ♠ 8 2
- ♡ J 9 5 2
- ◇ A Q 8 7
- ♣ 9 8 3

**South**
- ♠ A Q J 10 7 6 5 3
- ♡ 7 6
- ◇ —
- ♣ 7 5 2

| West | North | East | South |
|------|-------|------|-------|
|  |  | pass | 4♠ |
| pass | 5♣ | pass | 5◇ |
| pass | 7♠ | all pass |  |

West leads the ♣Q. Twelve tricks are easy – but where will the thirteenth come from?

Many bridge players rely on the Blackwood convention or one of the many variations of Blackwood whenever they are searching for a slam. However, on many hands, particularly very distributional hands, control-showing bids may provide the bidders with more useful information. Often these bids are called 'cuebids'.

On the illustrated deal, North-South can get to a grand slam by using control-showing bids. South's 4♠ bid indicates at least an eight-card spade suit, but not enough high card points for a one-level opening bid. Since North holds the ♠K, he should assume that South has the ♠A, and probably the ♠Q. Therefore it is reasonable for North to envision a slam with eight trump tricks, two club tricks, and two heart tricks, providing the defense cannot snatch the first two tricks in diamonds. North's 5♣ bid is a control-showing bid indicating first-round control of clubs, either the ♣A or a club void. The bid also shows slam interest with spades as trumps. It does not show a desire to make the club suit trumps since South's hand is known to be virtually useless in any contract other than spades. North can get very excited when South responds 5◇, indicating either the ◊A or more likely a diamond void. North can count thirteen tricks if South holds the ◊A. If instead South has a diamond void, declarer may still have thirteen top tricks since South might be holding the ♣Q or ♡Q or even a nine- rather than an eight-card spade suit. In any case, North can rationalize a quick prayer and the aggressive bid of 7♠.

When declarer sees the dummy he can count only twelve top tricks. The club loser is staring up at him. Declarer must try to develop a diamond winner in dummy in order to discard the club loser. Even though dummy's highest diamond is the lowly six, dummy does have five diamonds. With proper declarer play, and if East-West's diamonds break 4-4, the fifth diamond will become that much-needed winner.

It is necessary to play the diamond suit five times: four times to ruff and a fifth time to cash the winner. Therefore declarer needs five entries to dummy. Since declarer has exactly five entries to dummy, it is essential to use each entry to play a diamond from dummy. Therefore, when declarer wins the opening lead in dummy, he must play a diamond before playing trumps! If he plays even one round of trumps, he will find himself with one entry too few to establish and use the diamond winner. Notice that it was necessary to plan the play of the entire hand as soon as dummy appeared. This theme occurs very often throughout this book, but obviously it is a common theme in any book on declarer play.

The defenders may complain about their bad luck since the chance of their diamonds breaking 4-4 is only 33%. But declarer should be given credit for•appreciating the potential value of his five-card suit in dummy and putting in the hard work required to take advantage of a 4-4 split.

On hands where declarer has a singleton and dummy has five cards in that suit, the fifth card can be established if the defenders' seven cards split 4-3. The chance of this is a much better 62%.

Appreciate the potential of long suits. A small spot card can win a trick as easily as an ace if declarer can unleash its hidden power.

**Type of play:** Establish a long suit. Entry management.

**Inspirational features:**
1) Long suit in dummy is powerful even though it consists of only low spot cards.
2) Enough entries to dummy.
3) Slow loser in the club suit.

**Lose trick or do not try to win a trick:** Let's hope you will never have to use this technique when you are playing in a grand slam.

**Create deal exercise:** Modify this deal so that a trump finesse (successful of course) is required in order to have five entries to dummy.

## PROBLEM 5    CAN YOU BE A DETECTIVE?

Dealer North
East-West vul.

**North**
♠ 8 6 5
♡ K J 4 3 2
◇ Q 8 7
♣ J 7

**South**
♠ Q 9
♡ 7 6
◇ A K J 10 5 2
♣ K Q 10

| West | North | East | South |
|------|-------|------|-------|
|      | pass  | 1♠   | 2◇    |
| 2♠   | 3◇    | all pass |   |

West leads the ♠3. This contract depends on getting the hearts right. How are you going to play them and why?

## PROBLEM 6    YOU GO FIRST

Dealer West
Neither vul.

**North**
♠ Q 10 9 2
♡ J 7 5
◇ 9 7 6
♣ K 10 3

**South**
♠ A K J 8 7 3
♡ 4 3 2
◇ A
♣ A J 2

| West | North | East | South |
|------|-------|------|-------|
| pass | pass  | pass | 1♠    |
| pass | 2♠    | pass | 4♠    |
| all pass |   |      |       |

West leads the ◇K. How do you plan to find the ♣Q?

## PROBLEM 7 — WHO'S AFRAID OF THE BIG BAD RUFF?

Dealer West
Neither vul.

**North**
♠ A 4 2
♡ J 3
◇ 7 6 5
♣ 10 9 7 6 5

**South**
♠ K 5 3
♡ K Q 10 9 5 2
◇ A 3
♣ A 4

| West | North | East | South |
|------|-------|------|-------|
| 2♠ | pass | pass | 3♡ |
| all pass | | | |

West leads the ♠Q. Do you see any potential problems?

## PROBLEM 8 — YOU CAN COUNT ON IT

Dealer West
East-West vul.

**North**
♠ 9 6 3 2
♡ A 9
◇ A 10 4 2
♣ A 5 3

**South**
♠ 4
♡ K Q J 10 8 4
◇ K Q 3
♣ K 4 2

| West | North | East | South |
|------|-------|------|-------|
| 3♠ | pass | pass | 4♡ |
| pass | 6♡ | all pass | |

West leads the ♠A. You ruff the second spade, on which East discards. When you play hearts, West discards a spade on the second round. How will you continue from here?

**North**
♠ 8 6 5
♡ K J 4 3 2
♢ Q 8 7
♣ J 7

**West**
♠ J 7 3
♡ A 9 5
♢ 9 6
♣ 9 8 5 4 3

*Dealer N*
*EW Vul.*

**East**
♠ A K 10 4 2
♡ Q 10 8
♢ 4 3
♣ A 6 2

**South**
♠ Q 9
♡ 7 6
♢ A K J 10 5 2
♣ K Q 10

| West | North | East | South |
|------|-------|------|-------|
|  | pass | 1♠ | 2♢ |
| 2♠ | 3♢ | all pass |  |

West leads the ♠3. This contract depends on getting the hearts right. How are you going to play them and why?

Many top bridge players enjoy reading and even writing detective stories. This subject is not unrelated to declarer play in bridge. On many hands, a declarer has to be a detective in order to figure out which of the two defenders has a certain card.

On the illustrated deal, East won the first two spade tricks with the king and the ace, and on the third round of spades declarer ruffed. Since South must lose a club trick, the success of the contract depends on whether he can hold the heart losers to one. Eventually, South will have to lead a small heart and West will play low. At that point, declarer must decide whether to play the ♡J or ♡K. Which is the correct card to play?

In order to decide, consider how the ♡A and ♡Q can be divided between East and West. The following four cases cover all possibilities:

1) West has both the ace and the queen. Whether declarer plays the king or jack, the defense wins one heart trick and the contract succeeds.
2) East has both the ace and the queen. Whether declarer plays the king or jack, the defense wins two heart tricks and the contract fails.
3) West has the ace and East has the queen. If declarer plays the king, he loses one heart trick, but by playing the jack he loses two hearts.

4)  East has the ace and West has the queen. If declarer plays the jack, he loses one heart trick, but by playing the king he loses two hearts.

Clearly declarer can ignore cases 1 and 2 since the choice of play is irrelevant, so he should concern himself with whether case 3 or 4 is more likely. Since it is easier to locate an ace than a queen, it is best to try to figure out which defender is more likely to have the ace and assume the other opponent has the queen.

Upon seeing dummy, declarer can count 22 HCP in the North-South hands. He therefore knows East-West have a total of 18 HCP. Based on the bidding, it is clear the high card point division is probably East 12 or 13 and West 5 or 6.

By Trick 4 declarer has already seen East play the ♠AK (7 points) and West play the ♠J (1 point). At this time there are approximately 5 points remaining in East's hand and 5 points remaining in West's hand. Declarer still does not have enough information to decide which opponent has the ♡A. However, declarer can be quite certain that *neither opponent has both remaining aces.* Therefore declarer can pull trumps and play clubs until it is revealed which opponent has the ♣A. He will then assume with confidence that the other opponent has the crucial ♡A. On this hand, when East is forced to play his ♣A declarer will now assume case 3 and will successfully play a low heart to the king.

If the decision in hearts had been forced by an opening heart lead, declarer would not have had time to employ a discovery play. Declarer should assume that West did not underlead the ace and should therefore play the jack and pray.

When the detective (sorry, I mean 'declarer'!) makes a play for the purpose of obtaining information about the defenders' cards, it is called a **discovery play.** It can have the same effect as peeking at your opponent's cards, but it's good bridge rather than cheating.

**Type of play:** Discovery play. Card reading.

**Inspirational features:**
1)  Dummy's honors in the heart suit will eventually require a decision. (Card reading is clearly better than guessing.)
2)  Information gained from the bidding.
3)  The ability to delay the key decision until after declarer can gather all possible clues.

**Lose trick or do not try to win a trick:** Lose a trick to the ♣A prior to making the crucial heart decision.

**Create deal exercise:** Modify the East-West hands so that East's bid reveals that he does not have the ♡A and the discovery play is unnecessary.

**North**
- ♠ Q 10 9 2
- ♡ J 7 5
- ◇ 9 7 6
- ♣ K 10 3

**West**
- ♠ 5 4
- ♡ K 10 6
- ◇ K Q J 3
- ♣ Q 8 5 4

*Dealer W*
*Neither Vul.*

**East**
- ♠ 6
- ♡ A Q 9 8
- ◇ 10 8 5 4 2
- ♣ 9 7 6

**South**
- ♠ A K J 8 7 3
- ♡ 4 3 2
- ◇ A
- ♣ A J 2

| West | North | East | South |
|------|-------|------|-------|
| pass | pass | pass | 1♠ |
| pass | 2♠ | pass | 4♠ |
| all pass | | | |

West leads the ◇K. How do you plan to find the ♣Q?

Sorry, this was a trick question! The answer is that you should let the opponents find it for you. In the illustrated deal, South is eager to jump to 4♠ with his powerful hand. Declarer is looking at three heart losers and a possible club loser. The North-South clubs are a perfect example of a holding where you want the defenders to play the suit first. If declarer plays clubs first ('breaks' the club suit) he must decide which opponent to finesse for the queen. Before taking the club finesse, declarer can play a club winner hoping to drop a singleton queen: an extra but very unlikely possibility (1%). By then taking the finesse declarer has slightly better than a 50% chance of not losing a club trick. This is far superior to playing both the ace and king since the chance of dropping the queen doubleton is only 9%.

Declarer can avoid deciding how to finesse clubs by making the defenders break the suit. If either defender leads a club, declarer is certain to win three club tricks. On this hand declarer can achieve this by winning the opening lead, pulling trumps in two rounds ending in dummy, ruffing a diamond, returning to dummy with a trump, ruffing a second diamond and playing a heart. After the defenders take three heart tricks they will have to play either a heart, diamond, or club. If the defense plays a heart or a diamond, declarer can ruff in dummy and discard a club from his hand (called a 'ruff and a discard' or a 'ruff and sluff'). If the defender on lead plays a club, declarer will have achieved his goal of having the defense break the club suit. Either way the contract will succeed without declarer having to gamble on the club finesse.

It was necessary for declarer to ruff diamonds twice, or the defenders would have been able to play a diamond after winning the three heart tricks. The technique of ruffing out the diamonds in order to set up the ruff and sluff is called an **elimination** or **strip**.

In order to recognize endplays in the heat of battle at the bridge table, it is necessary to realize certain features that are usually present:
1) There is at least one suit that declarer wants the defenders to lead.
2) Declarer can prevent the defenders from having a safe card with which to exit their hands by stripping the hand, i.e., either drawing all cards in a suit out of their hands or setting up a ruff and a sluff.
3) In order for a ruff and a sluff to be successful, declarer cannot have any cards in the suit played by the defense in either his hand or dummy, and must have at least one trump in each hand.
4) Declarer must find an appropriate way to lose a trick to the defenders.

If the defense had taken three heart tricks before the hand was stripped, the endplay would not have been possible.

On the above deal you may have made your contract by guessing clubs correctly but I can assure you that you will find much greater happiness by achieving it through a strip and endplay.

**Type of play:** Endplay. Elimination (Strip).

**Inspirational features:**
1) A club suit that will eventually require guessing the queen's location, unless the defense leads a club.
2) Long trump length in both declarer and dummy.
3) The ability to eliminate the diamonds from dummy so that the diamond suit does not provide a safe exit for the defense.
4) A convenient way to lose a trick to the defense after the diamonds are eliminated.

**Lose trick or do not try to win a trick:** Playing a heart loser in order to put the defense on lead.

**Create deal exercise:** Modify this deal so that declarer holds the club queen instead of the jack but can still gain a trick via a strip and endplay.

**North**
- ♠ A 4 2
- ♡ J 3
- ◊ 7 6 5
- ♣ 10 9 7 6 5

**West**
- ♠ Q J 10 9 7 6
- ♡ A 8
- ◊ 10 9 8
- ♣ 8 3

Dealer W
Neither Vul.

**East**
- ♠ 8
- ♡ 7 6 4
- ◊ K Q J 4 2
- ♣ K Q J 2

**South**
- ♠ K 5 3
- ♡ K Q 10 9 5 2
- ◊ A 3
- ♣ A 4

| West | North | East | South |
|------|-------|------|-------|
| 2♠ | pass | pass | 3♡ |
| all pass | | | |

West leads the ♠Q. Do you see any potential problems?

Defenders usually get a sense of satisfaction when they are able to take a trick with a ruff. Sometimes, however, declarer will not be hurt if the defense gets a ruff. For example, if a defender holds the QJ10 in the trump suit, and if he can only ruff once, he will usually not profit by ruffing, since he has a natural trump trick. If he can ruff twice, that is a different story. Another situation where declarer does not mind a ruff is when a defender is ruffing a loser in declarer's hand.

On the illustrated deal, declarer is quite pleased by the dummy. There appears to be one loser in each suit and declarer will win the nine tricks required to make 3♡. But, before declarer plays a card from dummy on the first trick, he must realize that there is a potential threat. The weak two-bid by West usually implies a six-card suit, since West would normally open 3♠ with a seven-card suit and pass with a five-card suit. Therefore, declarer should assume that spades are breaking 6-1. Declarer must realize that West may also have the trump ace since he has only 3 HCP in the spade suit. The possibility of East getting a spade ruff is certainly real.

This information must all be digested by declarer on the first trick before he calls for a card from dummy, since the choice of that card will decide the fate of the contract. If declarer calls for the ♠A, he will be successful. After West wins a trump trick with the ace, he will probably lead the ♠J. If East ruffs this trick, declarer will play the remaining low spade from his hand – a card which is a loser in any case. If East does not ruff, declarer can win the trick in hand with the king. Whether East decides to ruff or not, declarer will win nine tricks.

Let us suppose declarer makes the mistake of winning the first trick with the ♠K. After West gains the lead with the trump ace, he will lead the ♠J. Declarer will have to make a play from dummy, either the ace or the remaining low spade, prior to East's play. If declarer plays the ace, East will ruff, and the defense will eventually win a second spade trick. If declarer plays the small spade, the ♠J will hold and East will happily wait to ruff the ace on the third round of spades. Either way the ruff will be painful for declarer, and the contract will be set.

The crucial point of this deal is that declarer must plan the play and recognize the threat before playing from dummy to the first trick. Since the North-South spade holding is not one that seems to require much thought, it is easy for declarer to let instinct and habit take control. If he blindly follows principles, such as, it is more natural to win in the fourth seat or it is desirable to keep the spade entry in dummy (dummy's only entry), declarer will be led astray.

When I am dummy and must place my hand on the table, the last suit I place on the table is the suit that has been led. I formed this habit to encourage my partner to look at the rest of my hand before thinking about that suit.

When you are declarer, particularly on the first trick, don't let the defense rush you; ignore any obvious signs of impatience through their body language. Bridge is not a track meet. The reward goes to the best player, not the fastest player.

**Type of play:** Ruffing air.

**Inspirational features:**
1) Awareness of the imminent threat of a spade ruff, due to West's 2♠ bid.
2) A slow loser in spades – the suit where the ruff will occur. Allow the defense to ruff that loser rather than a winner.

**Lose trick or do not try to win a trick:** Avoid being in the position of having to play a winner on a trick when a ruff might occur.

**Create deal exercise:** Modify this deal so that declarer is afraid of a spade ruff by West.

**North**
- ♠ 9 6 3 2
- ♡ A 9
- ◇ A 10 4 2
- ♣ A 5 3

**West**
- ♠ A K J 10 8 7 5
- ♡ 6
- ◇ J 9 7 6
- ♣ 9

Dealer W
EW Vul.

**East**
- ♠ Q
- ♡ 7 5 3 2
- ◇ 8 5
- ♣ Q J 10 8 7 6

**South**
- ♠ 4
- ♡ K Q J 10 8 4
- ◇ K Q 3
- ♣ K 4 2

| West | North | East | South |
|------|-------|------|-------|
| 3♠ | pass | pass | 4♡ |
| pass | 6♡ | all pass | |

West leads the ♠A. You ruff the second spade, on which East discards. When you play hearts, West discards a spade on the second round. How will you continue from here?

After a bridge hand is completed, one of the players may ask you if your shape was 4-5-3-1. Don't respond indignantly that you are a perfect 34-24-34. You are being asked in bridge shorthand if you were dealt 4 spades, 5 hearts, 3 diamonds, and 1 club. These four digits refer to the suits in reverse alphabetic order and of course always add up to 13. Sometime these numbers just refer to the number of cards in the suits without indicating specific suits. For example, a bridge player may describe a hand as a 4-3-3-3 distribution in order to indicate one four-card suit and three three-card suits. However, in this case, the four-card suit is not necessarily spades. *The Bridge World* magazine avoids this ambiguity by using the = symbol for the former interpretation.

On the illustrated deal the defense started with two rounds of spades. On the second trick East discarded a club and South ruffed. Now South attacked the trump suit. On the second round of trumps, West shed a spade. Only four tricks have been played, but an alert declarer has almost a complete knowledge of the distribution of the cards held by each defender, because each has already discarded. Since East had only one spade, West started with seven spades. This is consistent with the 3♠ bid. Since West started with only one heart, he had a total of five cards in clubs and diamonds. Declarer should continue playing trumps for two more rounds in order to remove East's trumps. Both West and dummy discard spades. If declarer continues by taking two rounds of clubs with the ace and king, a pleasant surprise occurs when West discards a spade on the second round: West started with exactly four diamonds and East with two. West's distribution is described as 7=1=4=1.

Using this information, declarer has no problem winning four diamond tricks. He first plays the ◊K and the ◊Q, exhausting East of his two diamonds, followed by leading the ◊3 in order to finesse with the ◊A10 combination. The fourth round of diamonds will enable declarer to discard his losing club.

Had West been able to follow to both rounds of clubs, declarer would have known that West started with at most three diamonds, and that it would be clearly wrong to finesse. Declarer would have had to hope that West had either three diamonds or the singleton or doubleton jack

The technique employed to figure out how many cards each defender has in each suit is called **counting.** It is important to recognize the situations when counting is needed. On the illustrated deal, declarer should foresee at the very first trick that he may eventually have to decide how to play the diamond suit. In this case (and most of the time) counting the hand provides the answer. This diamond suit combination is discussed in Appendix 1.

Even though it is very tiring to count hands when one first starts to play, it gets easier with experience. After all, since all players start with thirteen cards, once you know three suits, the fourth suit is revealed. Counting is essential for fine defense as well as declarer play. Good bridge players are rewarded for their effort.

**Type of play:** Counting the full hand (complete count). Card reading.

### Inspirational features:
1) The diamond suit will eventually require a decision.
2) If a defender shows out in a suit, the count of that suit is known.
3) When defenders show out in three suits, the complete count of all four suits is known. Here, declarer was certain diamonds were splitting 4-2 with West holding four.
4) Slow loser in clubs.

**Lose trick or do not try to win a trick:** —

**Create deal exercise:** Modify this deal so that declarer can be certain that diamonds are split 5-1 with West holding five and East one.

## PROBLEM 9    FIND THE WINNER IN DUMMY

Dealer: West
Both vul.

**North**
♠ 6 2
♡ 4 3 2
♢ 8 4 2
♣ 9 8 5 4 3

**South**
♠ A 5 3
♡ A K Q J 10 7
♢ A K 6
♣ 7

| West | North | East | South |
|------|-------|------|-------|
| 2♠ | pass | pass | 4♡ |
| all pass | | | |

West leads the ♠K. How are you going to secure your tenth trick?

## PROBLEM 10    A SIMPLE ADVANCED PLAY

Dealer: East
Neither vul.

**North**
♠ A 5 3 2
♡ A 5 2
♢ A Q J 3
♣ A K

**South**
♠ K Q 4
♡ K Q 4 3
♢ K 8 6 4
♣ Q 6

| West | North | East | South |
|------|-------|------|-------|
| | | pass | 1NT |
| pass | 7NT | all pass | |

West leads the ♣J. Plan the play.

## PROBLEM 11  WHEN THE WRONG WAY IS THE RIGHT WAY

Dealer: East
North-South vul.

**North**
♠ J 10 6 4 2
♡ A Q 5
◇ A 4 3
♣ J 5

**South**
♠ K Q 9 8 3
♡ K 9 8
◇ K J 9
♣ 10 9

| West | North | East | South |
|------|-------|------|-------|
|  |  | pass | 1♠ |
| 1NT[1] | 4♠ | all pass |  |

1. 16-18 HCP.

West leads the ♣A. With the unfortunate mirror pattern in the North-South
hands, there are no ruffs available, and clearly West has the ◇Q. So how do
you make 4♠?

## PROBLEM 12  TIMING IS EVERYTHING

Dealer: South
East-West vul.

**North**
♠ A J 8
♡ Q 10 8 5 2
◇ 7
♣ 7 5 4 2

**South**
♠ 5 3
♡ K J 9 6 4 3
◇ K Q 5
♣ A 6

| West | North | East | South |
|------|-------|------|-------|
|  |  |  | 1♡ |
| pass | 4♡ | all pass |  |

West leads the ♠K. It looks as though your club loser can eventually be
parked on the ♠J — do you see any pitfalls that may affect your line of play?

**North**
- ♠ 6 2
- ♡ 4 3 2
- ◊ 8 4 2
- ♣ 9 8 5 4 3

**West**
- ♠ K Q J 9 7 4
- ♡ 9
- ◊ 9 7 3
- ♣ K 10 2

Dealer W
Both Vul.

**East**
- ♠ 10 8
- ♡ 8 6 5
- ◊ Q J 10 5
- ♣ A Q J 6

**South**
- ♠ A 5 3
- ♡ A K Q J 10 7
- ◊ A K 6
- ♣ 7

| West | North | East | South |
|------|-------|------|-------|
| 2♠ | pass | pass | 4♡ |
| all pass | | | |

West leads the ♠K. How are you going to secure your tenth trick?

A bridge player can describe his hand as a **yarborough** if it does not have a single card that is higher than a nine. Such a hand is very rare. Legend has it that the Earl of Yarborough offered odds of 1000 to 1 against a player being dealt such a hand. This was a very favorable bet for the Earl since the actual odds against such a hand is 1827 to 1. The method for obtaining these odds is explained in Appendix 1. Many bridge players use the term yarborough to describe a weak hand even if it does not satisfy the above condition.

On the illustrated deal, North has a true yarborough. South should feel confident about the 4♡ bid since he is looking at nine top tricks and needs only to find one winning trick in dummy. Unfortunately dummy's yarborough means declarer must search for that winner. Clearly using a trump for a ruff in dummy is the only possibility. Declarer should realize, however, that trying to ruff a spade before pulling trumps will only result in an overruff by East. After all, West's weak two-bid in spades almost guarantees that he has six spades and East has only two. Most players do not open weak two-bids with five-card suits and they tend to preempt at the three-level with seven-card suits.

Declarer should also realize that playing two rounds of trumps before ruffing a spade in dummy is very likely to be unsuccessful. If declarer has no information about the distribution of the defender's hands the chance of East having three or four hearts is 30%. On this particular deal, since declarer should assume spades are breaking 6-2, the chance of East having three or four hearts rises to 49%.

The best possibility for declarer is to maneuver to ruff a diamond instead! Declarer can win the opening lead and continue with a small spade at the second trick. After declarer regains the lead, declarer should play a third spade but must resist the desire to ruff in dummy since East will overruff. On that third spade declarer should discard a diamond from dummy. Now when declarer regains the lead he can cash two top trumps, cash the ◇AK if the defense has not already forced declarer to play these cards, play the ◇6 and ruff in dummy. East will still have a trump but with luck he will not be able to overruff the third round of diamonds.

This play will only succeed if East was dealt four or more diamonds (but he is known to have at least eight cards in the minor suits). It will fail if East started with only three diamonds since he can throw a diamond on the same trick on which declarer discards a diamond from dummy. There are many such similar situations where declarer can gain by playing a loser in one hand and throwing a loser from another suit in the other hand.

Notice that it would be a mistake for declarer to play even one round of trumps before playing the losing spades. If declarer had done this, East could win the second spade trick and play a second round of trumps. West could win the third spade (the trick on which dummy discards a diamond), get to East with a club, and East could play his remaining heart and remove the last trump from dummy. Therefore if declarer pulls even one round of trumps, the defense can prevent the loser-on-loser play from producing that one important trick needed from dummy.

**Type of play:** Loser-on-loser. Trump management.

**Inspirational features:**
1) Fear of being overruffed by East when trying to ruff a spade.
2) A diamond suit where a loser can be discarded thereby allowing a ruff in that suit.
3) Slow loser in diamonds — a trick that cannot be cashed by the defense when West wins the third round of spades.

**Lose trick or do not try to win a trick:** Don't try to ruff the spade loser.

**Create deal exercise:** Modify the deal so that West opened the bidding 3♠ but the same loser-on-loser play is required.

**North**
♠ A 5 3 2
♡ A 5 2
♢ A Q J 3
♣ A K

**West**
♠ 7
♡ 7 6
♢ 10 9 5
♣ J 10 9 7 5 3 2

Dealer E
Neither Vul.

**East**
♠ J 10 9 8 6
♡ J 10 9 8
♢ 7 2
♣ 8 4

**South**
♠ K Q 4
♡ K Q 4 3
♢ K 8 6 4
♣ Q 6

| West | North | East | South |
|------|-------|------|-------|
|      |       | pass | 1NT   |
| pass | 7NT   | all pass |   |

West leads the ♣J. Plan the play.

Once North recuperated from the surprise that South had enough points to open 1NT, he had an easy time jumping straight to 7NT. After all if their 1NT range is 15-17 HCP, North is certain they have at least 37 points.

However, when declarer saw the high card laden dummy, he was somewhat disappointed. Unfortunately there are only twelve top tricks. There are two obvious ways of winning a thirteenth trick. All declarer needs is either the hearts to break 3-3 or the spades to break 3-3. There is also a third possibility: a squeeze play. Suppose neither hearts nor spades break 3-3, then only one defender will have four or more hearts. This defender's job will be to keep four hearts. Likewise, if spades don't split 3-3, only one defender will have four or more spades. This defender's job will be to keep four spades. Suppose the same defender has to do both jobs, that is keep four hearts and four spades. In the illustrated hand, East has both jobs. Suppose declarer cashes his two top clubs and three top diamonds. On these five tricks East can comfortably play his four minor-suit cards and discard a spade. The following is the position when the ♢J is led to the sixth trick:

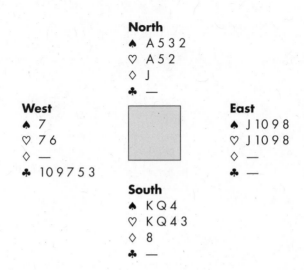

**North**
- ♠ A 5 3 2
- ♡ A 5 2
- ◇ J
- ♣ —

**West**
- ♠ 7
- ♡ 7 6
- ◇ —
- ♣ 10 9 7 5 3

**East**
- ♠ J 10 9 8
- ♡ J 10 9 8
- ◇ —
- ♣ —

**South**
- ♠ K Q 4
- ♡ K Q 4 3
- ◇ 8
- ♣ —

East must throw one of his four hearts or one of his four remaining spades. The fourth heart in declarer's hand and the fourth spade in dummy are both threat cards. We see that East has two jobs on this hand, but cannot successfully do both. The same squeeze would operate if West were the player who has to keep both the major suits guarded. Of course declarer would not make 7NT if East had been dealt four or more cards in one major and West four or more cards in the other major. But good bridge is about giving yourself every possibility to make your contract.

In order to learn how to find a squeeze play at the table it is necessary to study the technique rather than merely see a few examples. If you would like to learn about squeeze execution, I would, of course, strongly recommend my book *A Bridge to Simple Squeezes* (Master Point Press, 2nd. ed., 2007).

**Type of play:** Simple squeeze.

**Inspirational features:**
1) Possessing a 4-3 fit in a suit that contains the ace, king, and queen and realizing that the fourth card can put pressure on a defender to keep four cards in that suit. (In my book on simple squeezes, I label that fourth card a **strong threat card** since only one defender can prevent it from winning a trick.)
2) Twelve top tricks.

**Lose trick or do not try to win a trick:** —

**Create deal exercise:** Modify this deal so that North has four-card suits in both majors. (This time the squeeze will only work against West.)

**North**
- ♠ J 10 6 4 2
- ♡ A Q 5
- ◊ A 4 3
- ♣ J 5

**West**
- ♠ A 7
- ♡ J 10 2
- ◊ Q 7 6
- ♣ A K Q 8 6

*Dealer E*
*NS Vul.*

**East**
- ♠ 5
- ♡ 7 6 4 3
- ◊ 10 8 5 2
- ♣ 7 4 3 2

**South**
- ♠ K Q 9 8 3
- ♡ K 9 8
- ◊ K J 9
- ♣ 10 9

| West | North | East | South |
|------|-------|------|-------|
|      |       | pass | 1♠    |
| 1NT[1] | 4♠  | all pass |  |

1. 16-18 HCP.

West leads the ♣A. With the unfortunate mirror pattern in the North-South hands, there are no ruffs available, and clearly West has the ◊Q. So how do you make 4♠?

Early in his bridge career, the novice is shown how to take a finesse. The fledgling player feels a sense of accomplishment learning a technique with such an impressive name. After all 'finesse' is defined in the non-bridge world as 'delicate manipulation, subtle discrimination, artfulness, and cunning strategy'. In the world of bridge, however, a finesse is a very common basic play and taking a finesse will not create any adulation from a kibitzer. Actually one later learns many advanced plays, such as a strip and endplay, that are made with the intent of avoiding a finesse, an example of which occurred in Problem 6.

A finesse is even more irresistible when the adjective 'free' is placed in front of it. In Problem 3, however, we saw how disastrously a free finesse can turn out. In Problem 15, we will see an **obligatory finesse**. That will live up to its name: it must be taken.

On the illustrated deal one encounters an unusual finesse. West grabbed the first three tricks with the ♣AK and the trump ace. On the fourth trick West played the ♠7. The only possible additional loser for declarer is a diamond trick. The normal play of the diamond suit is to cash the ace and then play toward the king and the jack, taking a finesse with the jack. On this hand, though, the normal play is clearly wrong. The North-South hands have a combined total of 24 high-card-points. Since West was kind enough to announce that he has 16-18 HCP, West must have the ◊Q, and the normal finesse will lose.

In order to make the contract declarer must take a rather unusual diamond finesse. Since West is known to have the queen, declarer should play diamonds by first leading the jack from the South hand. If West does not cover with the queen, declarer will just let the jack ride and it will win the trick. If West covers, which he probably will, declarer can win with the ace and then play a diamond from the dummy toward the ◊K9, taking a finesse against the ◊10 with the ◊9.

This unusual technique for playing the diamond suit is called a **backward finesse**. It requires two cards to be placed properly, the ◊Q with West and the ◊10 with East. Without any information about the defenders' holdings, the chance of success is only about 25%. On the above hand the bidding provided declarer with the information that the standard finesse had no chance of success while the backward finesse had better than a 60% chance of success. The 1NT overcall placed all the missing high cards with West. Since East has no picture cards, he has the majority of the spot cards.

If South had not held the ◊9, declarer's only line of play consistent with West's 1NT bid would have been to play the ◊AK and hope West held queen doubleton.

Unless declarer has extra information that indicates a backward finesse is called for, he should not attempt it. It is the wrong way to play the suit. If you are a fine player and you take a backward finesse for no apparent reason, your opponents will wonder if you peeked at their cards.

**Type of play:** Backward finesse. Card reading.

**Inspirational features:**
1) The normal diamond finesse cannot be successful after West's bid, but a backward finesse may avoid the diamond loser.
2) The ◊9 in the South hand.

**Lose trick or do not try to win a trick:** —

**Create deal exercise:** Modify this deal so that the defense holds ◊A, ◊J and ◊9 where a backward finesse is necessary to limit the number of losers in this suit to one.

**North**
- ♠ A J 8
- ♡ Q 10 8 5 2
- ◇ 7
- ♣ 7 5 4 2

**West**
- ♠ K Q 7
- ♡ 7
- ◇ A 10 4 3 2
- ♣ 10 9 8 3

*Dealer S*
*EW Vul.*

**East**
- ♠ 10 9 6 4 2
- ♡ A
- ◇ J 9 8 6
- ♣ K Q J

**South**
- ♠ 5 3
- ♡ K J 9 6 4 3
- ◇ K Q 5
- ♣ A 6

| West | North | East | South |
|------|-------|------|-------|
| | | | 1♡ |
| pass | 4♡ | all pass | |

West leads the ♠K. It looks as though your club loser can eventually be parked on the ♠J — do you see any pitfalls if you take this line of play?

A major goal of bidding is to enable a partnership to find its best trump fit. Another important goal, particularly at duplicate bridge, is to make it difficult for the opponents to find their best trump fit. This becomes very significant when a partnership has an excellent fit since it implies that the opponents also have at least one very good fit. Suppose a partnership finds a ten-card fit in spades, then its opponents have only three spades and twenty-three cards in clubs, diamonds, and hearts. Therefore the opponents must have either at least a nine-card fit or two eight-card fits.

On the illustrated deal, North's jump to 4♡ is an example of a bid that may work out well even if declarer cannot make the contract since the bid may prevent the opponents from finding their fit. The 4♡ bid indicates a weak hand with five- or six-card trump support and a void or singleton in a side suit. This bid should not be made with more than 9 HCP. Other bids are available to North to describe a good hand with heart support.

Declarer won the opening lead with the ♠A and led trumps. After East won with the ♡A, he played the ♣K driving out South's ace. Declarer was confident that West had the ♠Q since the ♠K was the opening lead. He therefore played the ♠5 toward the ♠J setting up a club discard. Of course it was too late; after the defense won the spade trick they immediately took both a club and a diamond trick dooming the contract.

Declarer lamented, 'Bad timing. If only I could have gotten to my hand to play a spade toward the jack before my ace of clubs was driven out, I would have been able to discard my club loser. Bridge is a cruel game.'

South was correct in his analysis that in order to make the contract he had to lose a spade trick while he still held the ♣A. Declarer overlooked the fact that he could have accomplished this on the first trick: simply let West win with the ♠K. Whatever the defense does now, the contract is safe. If West now shifts to a club to drive out the ace, on the third trick South can play a spade toward the ♠AJ, finessing against the ♠Q with confidence. This would enable declarer to discard the club loser at Trick 4 before giving up the lead to the opponents.

In many situations in bridge, as well as in life, success or failure depends on timing. Sometimes bad timing is thrust upon us by fate. On this hand, however, declarer was too quick to blame fate. Remember that the time to think about timing is on the first trick.

**Type of play:** Ducking. Timing. Entry management.

**Inspirational features:**
1) The lead indicated the location of the ♠Q.
2) Losing a spade trick will create a winner with the marked spade finesse.
3) Slow loser in clubs cannot be cashed by the defense, unless declarer has used the ♣A as an entry.
4) The only immediate entry to South is the ♣A.

**Lose trick or do not try to win a trick:** Ducking the opening lead sets up an additional spade trick before the ♣A is driven out.

**Create deal exercise:** Modify the deal so that West has the ♠Q and ♠J, South has the ♠K, and when West leads the ♠Q, South must win the first trick with the ♠K and then take a spade finesse on the second trick.

Dealer: East
North-South vul.

**North**
♠ K Q J 9
♡ 8 4 3
◇ A K 5 3
♣ K 5

**South**
♠ A 10 8 7 4 3
♡ 7 6 5
◇ 6 4 2
♣ A

| West | North | East | South |
|------|-------|------|-------|
|      |       | pass | 2♠ |
| pass | 2NT | pass | 3♠ |
| pass | 4♠ | all pass | |

West leads the ♠6. You have an easy ten tricks, but you are playing matchpoints. Do you see any chance to do better?

Dealer: West
East-West vul.

**North**
♠ 9 6 5
♡ K 7 6 4 3
◇ 6
♣ A 8 4 2

**South**
♠ J 4 2
♡ A 9 8 5 2
◇ A 7 4 2
♣ J

| West | North | East | South |
|------|-------|------|-------|
| pass | pass | 1◇ | 1♡ |
| 1NT | 4♡ | all pass | |

West leads the ♡Q and East discards on this trick. Can you make the contract with this bad trump break?

## PROBLEM 15  SHOULD YOU BE AN OPTIMIST OR A PESSIMIST?

Dealer: West
Both vul.

**North**
- ♠ J 5 3
- ♡ J 10 5
- ◇ K 5 3
- ♣ K 6 4 2

**South**
- ♠ 7 6 2
- ♡ A K Q
- ◇ Q 7 6 4 2
- ♣ A 7

| West | North | East | South |
|------|-------|------|-------|
| pass | pass | pass | 1NT |
| pass | 2NT | all pass | |

West starts off with the ♠A. Do you see any hope of winning eight tricks?

## PROBLEM 16  FORCE YOUR OPPONENTS TO HELP YOU

Dealer: North
Both vul.

**North**
- ♠ A 8 4
- ♡ 5 2
- ◇ J 9 5 4
- ♣ J 7 4 2

**South**
- ♠ 7 5 3 2
- ♡ A Q 4
- ◇ A K Q
- ♣ A K Q

| West | North | East | South |
|------|-------|------|-------|
| | pass | pass | 2♣ |
| pass | 2◇ | pass | 2NT |
| pass | 3NT | all pass | |

West leads the ♠K, and that cuts you off from both minor-suit jacks in dummy. You can win the ♠A and take a heart finesse — but perhaps there is something better?

**North**
- ♠ K Q J 9
- ♡ 8 4 3
- ◇ A K 5 3
- ♣ K 5

**West**
- ♠ 6 5
- ♡ K J 9
- ◇ Q 9 8
- ♣ Q 10 6 3 2

*Dealer E*
*NS Vul.*

**East**
- ♠ 2
- ♡ A Q 10 2
- ◇ J 10 7
- ♣ J 9 8 7 4

**South**
- ♠ A 10 8 7 4 3
- ♡ 7 6 5
- ◇ 6 4 2
- ♣ A

| West | North | East | South |
|------|-------|------|-------|
| | | pass | 2♠ |
| pass | 2NT | pass | 3♠ |
| pass | 4♠ | all pass | |

West leads the ♠6. You have an easy ten tricks, but you are playing matchpoints. Do you see any chance to do better?

Even though virtually all duplicate players use weak two-bids, there is little consensus regarding which hands justify a weak two-bid. Some experts feel that the weak two-bidder must have a six-card suit. Others will happily open in third seat with only a five-card suit. Some will open in any seat with a five-card suit. One should also consider vulnerability, suit quality, and whether the event is matchpoints or teams.

The main advantage of only requiring a five-card suit in order to open a weak two-bid is that you have more opportunities to open at the two-level and thereby interfere with your opponents' ability to get to their best contract. The main disadvantage occurs when the partner of the weak two-bidder has a good hand and is considering going to game in a suit or notrump, since he cannot tell whether the weak two-bidder has a five- or six-card suit. This problem is particularly significant when the responder has a big hand but only one or two cards in partner's suit. One approach to this problem is to play the following modified form of **Ogust**. If the weak two-bid shows either a five- or six-card suit and 5-10 points, the responses to 2NT don't indicate a feature, but are as follows:

3♣: 5-7 points with a 5-card suit,

3◊: 8-10 points with a 5-card suit,

3♡: 5-7 points with a 6-card suit,

3♠: 8-10 points with a 6-card suit,

3NT: Solid running 6-card suit.

On the illustrated deal, when playing this modified Ogust, it is reasonable for North to bid 4♠ if South's response to 2NT is either 3◊ or 3♠. North should bid only 3♠ if South's response is either 3♣ or 3♡.

The opening trump lead allowed declarer to pull trumps, and discard a heart loser on the second round of clubs. Declarer made 4♠ since he lost only two heart tricks and one diamond trick. After the hand, the defense mistakenly thought they could have defeated the contract if they had led hearts, but declarer pointed out that if the defense had taken their three heart tricks, he would have been able to throw the diamond loser on the ♣K. Declarer felt the lead was of no importance.

Actually the lead was a gift, but declarer was too eager to discard a heart on dummy's winning club and never took advantage of the favorable lead. Instead, South should have discarded a diamond on the second round of clubs. Then declarer could have played the ◊A and ◊K and ruffed the third round. If diamonds break 3-3, as they did on this hand, declarer can return to dummy with a trump and discard a heart on the fourth diamond in dummy. The chance of diamonds breaking 3-3 is only 36%, but since there is no risk involved why not play for the extra trick? At duplicate bridge these are the plays that separate the winning players from the rest of the field.

This is a rare hand where declarer should discard a slow loser rather than a fast one, by discarding a diamond on the ♣K rather than a heart.

When you have an opportunity to discard a loser, don't just look for the most obvious loser or the one closest to your thumb and forefinger, but consider which is the best loser to discard. It does make a difference.

**Type of play:** Establish a long suit.

**Inspirational features:**
1) The ♣K can be used to discard either a diamond or a heart.
2) Fourth diamond in North is a potential winner for a heart discard.

**Lose trick or do not try to win a trick:** —

**Create deal exercise:** Modify this deal so that two heart losers can be discarded.

**North**
- ♠ 9 6 5
- ♡ K 7 6 4 3
- ◇ 6
- ♣ A 8 4 2

**West**
- ♠ K 8 7
- ♡ Q J 10
- ◇ 10 9 5
- ♣ K 7 6 5

Dealer W
EW Vul.

**East**
- ♠ A Q 10 3
- ♡ —
- ◇ K Q J 8 3
- ♣ Q 10 9 3

**South**
- ♠ J 4 2
- ♡ A 9 8 5 2
- ◇ A 7 4 2
- ♣ J

| West | North | East | South |
|------|-------|------|-------|
| pass | pass | 1◇ | 1♡ |
| 1NT | 4♡ | all pass | |

West leads the ♡Q and East discards on this trick. Can you make the contract with this bad trump break?

In a notrump contract, declarer should usually be focusing on how many winning tricks are immediately available or could be developed. One must not, however, totally ignore losing tricks. Even when declarer is considering ways of developing more winning tricks, he must be aware of the number of tricks the defense can grab.

In a suit contract, declarer will usually spend most of his energy counting losing tricks rather than winning tricks. An exception occurs when a line of play involves crossruffing where it is often best to count how many winning tricks are available.

On the illustrated deal, declarer showed his hand after the first trick, while stating, 'Down one. I have four losing tricks; one trump trick and three spade tricks. I have no way of discarding spade losers but I can ruff my clubs and diamonds. Too bad the trump suit did not break 2-1, I would have made the contract.' Declarer was proud to show his ability to count losing tricks.

Declarer should, however, consider the following line of play that would have won him eight heart tricks and two aces for ten tricks. He could win the ace and king of trumps, ♣A, club ruff, ◇A, diamond ruff, club ruff, diamond ruff, club ruff, and diamond ruff. West could ruff the fourth round of diamonds, but if he does declarer will discard a spade from dummy and eventually win a tenth trick by ruffing one of South's spades in dummy. Declarer's only fear should be that West can overruff a round of clubs. Note that it is essential for declarer to start with a club ruff rather than a diamond ruff and to ruff the fourth club prior to the fourth diamond in order to prevent West from discarding a club on the fourth round of diamonds and overruffing the fourth round of clubs.

Some readers might find a paradox on this deal, since declarer can count four losing tricks and ten winning tricks when there are only thirteen tricks! The solution to this puzzle is that declarer made the four losers collide on three tricks. This collision occurs whether West chooses to ruff a diamond or not. If he doesn't ruff, after declarer wins the first ten tricks, three losing spades will remain in both the North and South hands, and West will end up using his high trump on one of these last three tricks. If West does ruff a diamond, a spade loser will be discarded from dummy. Note that if the defense had taken the first three spade tricks, the contract would have been doomed.

Remember to count winners on crossruff hands.

**Type of play:** Crossruff.

**Inspirational features:**
1) Long trump length in both declarer's hand and dummy.
2) Shortness in different side suits.
3) Lack of a side suit that can be established.

**Lose trick or do not try to win a trick:** –

**Create deal exercise:** Modify the East-West cards so that declarer must start with a diamond ruff in order to prevent East from overruffing a diamond.

**North**
- ♠ J 5 3
- ♡ J 10 5
- ◇ K 5 3
- ♣ K 6 4 2

**West**
- ♠ A K Q 10
- ♡ 4 3
- ◇ J 10 8
- ♣ 10 8 5 3

*Dealer W*
*Both Vul.*

**East**
- ♠ 9 8 4
- ♡ 9 8 7 6 2
- ◇ A 9
- ♣ Q J 9

**South**
- ♠ 7 6 2
- ♡ A K Q
- ◇ Q 7 6 4 2
- ♣ A 7

| West | North | East | South |
|------|-------|------|-------|
| pass | pass | pass | 1NT |
| pass | 2NT | all pass | |

West starts off with the ♠A. Do you see any hope of winning eight tricks?

When an expert player becomes declarer in a contract that is likely to be successful, he will become a pessimist. Declarer will imagine an undesirable location of the East-West cards (for example, a bad trump break) where some reasonable lines of play may fail. He will then try to choose a line of play that will be successful even with this unlikely lie of the cards.

When an expert player is declarer in a contract that seems likely to fail, he will become an optimist. Declarer will imagine a favorable location of the East-West cards which will allow the contract to be successful. He will then play the hand under the assumption that the cards are placed in that lucky fashion.

On the illustrated deal, declarer is in 2NT after North invited him to go to game. Since South opened with a minimum hand for a 1NT bid, and North had a minimum hand for an invitation, declarer finds himself in a difficult 2NT contract.

The defense wins the first four tricks by running the spade suit. On the fourth round of spades a heart is discarded from both North and East and a diamond from South. West leads a club on the fifth trick. Declarer has to decide where to win the club, and how to play the diamond suit.

Since declarer has already lost four tricks it is necessary to play diamonds in such a way as to not lose more than one trick. Declarer must now be an optimist and envision a distribution of the East-West diamonds where this is possible. His only hope is to assume that one defender has specifically ace doubleton and that he can properly guess which defender that is.

On this hand declarer does not have to guess which defender has the ◇A. During the bidding West elected to pass with the ace, king, and queen of spades, so it is clear East was dealt the ◇A. Therefore, declarer must be an optimist and assume East has the ace doubleton. Based on this assumption, declarer should win the club trick with the king in dummy in order to play the ◇3 from North. After East correctly plays the ◇9, declarer wins this trick with the ◇Q. Then declarer can play the ◇4 from his hand and the ◇5 from dummy, while praying that East will have to play the ace on this trick. When the ◇A hits the table a relieved, smiling and unfortunately probably gloating declarer can claim the rest of the tricks. Declarer needed good luck, good technique and an optimistic approach in order to succeed in this 2NT contract. The second round of diamonds, when a low card is played from both declarer and dummy, is called an **obligatory finesse.**

Since on this hand South was certain East held the ◇A, the probability of finding East with ace doubleton was 27%. If declarer had to guess which defender held the ◇A and whom to play for ace doubleton, the probability of success would be cut in half to 13.5%. At times declarer must be an optimist and assume it is the actual situation.

This is an example of bridge offering a lesson in life. When one finds oneself in a difficult situation, one must be an optimist and envision a positive outcome.

**Type of play:** Obligatory finesse. Card reading. Assumption.

**Inspirational features:**
1) Difficult contracts require an optimistic declarer.
2) Must assume a possible holding for the defenders in the diamond suit so that there is only one loser.
3) Knowledge of the location of the ◇A.

**Lose trick or do not try to win a trick:** Don't try to win the second round of the diamond suit with the king. If West held the ace not only would he have had an opening bid but he would have used it to capture the queen on the first round of the suit.

**Create deal exercise:** Modify the deal so that both North and South have four diamonds.

**North**
♠ A 8 4
♡ 5 2
◇ J 9 5 4
♣ J 7 4 2

**West**
♠ K Q J 10 6
♡ K 8
◇ 10 6 3 2
♣ 9 3

*Dealer N*
*Both Vul.*

**East**
♠ 9
♡ J 10 9 7 6 3
◇ 8 7
♣ 10 8 6 5

**South**
♠ 7 5 3 2
♡ A Q 4
◇ A K Q
♣ A K Q

| West | North | East | South |
|------|-------|------|-------|
|      | pass  | pass | 2♣    |
| pass | 2◇    | pass | 2NT   |
| pass | 3NT   | all pass |   |

West leads the ♠K, and that cuts you off from both the minor-suit jacks in dummy. You can win the ♠A and take a heart finesse — but perhaps there is something better?

Once upon a time bridge players used strong two-bids. Opening bids of two of a suit indicated an extremely strong hand with length in that suit. At that time, a 2NT opening bid was used to describe a balanced hand with 22-24 high card points (HCP). As the world became less civilized, duplicate bridge players switched over to weak two-bids. When playing weak two-bids, the 2♣ opening bid becomes a multi-purpose artificial bid to describe all very strong hands. This treatment enables players to show a balanced 22-24 point hand by making an opening bid of 2♣ and then rebidding 2NT. The opening 2NT bid now indicates a 20-21 HCP hand.

When a player makes a bid showing 22-24 HCP it is much more likely that his hand contains 22 points than 24 points. The chance that the hand will hold 22 points is 55%, 23 points is 30%, and 24 points is only 15%. If you don't believe these values, please check Appendix 1. These percentages may seem surprising, but remember that the average hand has 10 HCP. The further the point count of a hand is from 10, the less likely it is that the hand will occur. This principle can even be observed on a 1NT opening bid. The results are not as dramatic, but when playing a 15-17 HCP range, the chances of holding 15, 16 or 17 HCP are 44%, 33% and 23% respectively. Use of this principle may help the other three players with decisions at the bridge table, but since each player will have knowledge of his own hand, the probabilities have to be modified. The point pattern indicated by the principle will still be applicable. Some years back, most duplicate players shifted their 1NT range from 16-18 to 15-17. This greatly increased the frequency of opening 1NT.

On the illustrated deal, the opening lead of the ♠K is painful for declarer. If any other suit had been led, declarer would have had ten top tricks: four clubs, four diamonds, one heart and one spade. Unfortunately, the ♠A is a precious entry to dummy, and once it is played declarer will no longer be able to get there to cash dummy's two jacks. Declarer should duck the ♠K of course — after all, maybe West will foolishly shift to a different suit. However, any sober defender will continue spades and declarer should duck until he has to play the ace on the third round.

Declarer has only eight winning tricks. One way to try to win a ninth trick is to take a heart finesse. By ducking spades, declarer learned that suit was split 5-1. Since declarer knows that West has only eight cards that are not spades and East started with twelve cards that were not spades, the chance of the heart finesse being successful is a nice 60%.

Declarer, however, should resist the temptation of the heart finesse since with proper play the 3NT contract cannot fail. South should proceed by cashing his three top clubs and three top diamonds. Declarer should then play a spade. After winning that trick, West can cash his last spade winner. This eleventh trick will leave dummy with the two jacks as his last two cards, and South with the ♡AQ. Now if West plays a club or diamond the dummy wins the last two tricks. If West plays a heart South wins the last two tricks.

This deal is an example of an **endplay.** Declarer forced West into doing what declarer could not accomplish on his own.

**Type of play:** Endplay. Entry management. Unblocking.

**Inspirational features:**
1) Heart suit that has two sure winners if West can be forced to lead it.
2) Lack of an entry to dummy.
3) West cannot take enough spades to defeat the contract.

**Lose trick or do not try to win a trick:** Lose spade tricks to put the defense on lead.

**Create deal exercise:** Modify this deal so that the endplay will only be successful when West has the ♡K.

Dealer: East
Both vul.

**North**
♠ 8 7 4
♡ 5 4
◊ A Q 7 6 5 3
♣ 5 3

**South**
♠ A K 3
♡ A K 3 2
◊ J 4
♣ A K 4 2

| West | North | East | South |
|------|-------|------|-------|
|      |       | pass | 2NT   |
| pass | 3NT   | all pass |   |

West leads the ♠Q, and you have seven top tricks. The rest can only come from diamonds, so how do you plan to produce them?

Dealer: West
Neither vul.

**North**
♠ Q J 9 4
♡ A J 10 8 5
◊ 6 2
♣ A 4

**South**
♠ A K 10 8
♡ K Q 2
◊ 8 4 3
♣ 7 5 2

| West | North | East | South |
|------|-------|------|-------|
| pass | 1♡    | pass | 1♠    |
| pass | 2♠    | pass | 4♡    |
| pass | 4♠    | all pass |   |

Would you prefer to be declarer in 4♠ or 4♡ on this deal? Is there a general conclusion you can draw from your answer?

Dealer: West
Neither vul.

**North**
♠ 8 2
♡ K 9 8 7
◇ J 7 6 4
♣ A Q 5

**South**
♠ A K 4
♡ A 10 5
◇ Q 10 9 8 5
♣ K 7

| West | North | East | South |
|------|-------|------|-------|
| 2♠ | pass | pass | 2NT |
| pass | 3NT | all pass | |

West leads the ♠Q, of course. How do you intend to set up diamonds without allowing the defense to cash too many spade winners?

Dealer: West
Both vul.

**North**
♠ 8 7 6
♡ A 4
◇ A J 10 4 3
♣ K 7 6

**South**
♠ A Q 5
♡ Q 2
◇ K Q 9 5
♣ 10 9 8 5

| West | North | East | South |
|------|-------|------|-------|
| pass | 1◇ | pass | 3NT |
| all pass | | | |

West leads the ♡J, you play low from dummy, and your queen wins. First hurdle safely passed! How will you play from here?

**North**
♠ 8 7 4
♡ 5 4
◇ A Q 7 6 5 3
♣ 5 3

**West**
♠ Q J 10 6 5
♡ Q 9
◇ K 10 2
♣ 9 8 6

Dealer E
Both Vul.

**East**
♠ 9 2
♡ J 10 8 7 6
◇ 9 8
♣ Q J 10 7

**South**
♠ A K 3
♡ A K 3 2
◇ J 4
♣ A K 4 2

| West | North | East | South |
|------|-------|------|-------|
|      |       | pass | 2NT |
| pass | 3NT | all pass | |

West leads the ♠Q, and you have seven top tricks. The rest can only come from diamonds, so how do you plan to produce them?

One of the many attractive features of bridge is that it is an excellent mix of skill and luck. A game that is pure luck is not very enjoyable – roulette tables and slot machines in casinos would be empty were it not for the excitement generated by the prospect of winning and losing money. By contrast, games of pure skill tend to have very predictable results. Thirty thousand runners might take part in the New York marathon, but fewer than a dozen have any chance of winning the overall event.

In duplicate bridge, there is still a wonderful mix of skill and luck. Skill plays a large role in determining the success of the players, but luck is still a factor. Consider a deal where most East-West pairs play in a reasonable contract of 4♠; due to a lucky lie of the cards, three finesses are successful and declarer wins twelve tricks. Now suppose the East-West pair that your partnership plays against overbids and winds up in the very bad contract of 6♠. Due to their good luck and your bad luck they get an undeserved excellent result and you get a terrible one.

Usually declarer feels lucky when he takes a winning finesse. On the illustrated deal, however, declarer might profit from losing a finesse.

It is necessary to win at least three diamond tricks in order for declarer to make 3NT. When South plays the ◊J in order to take a diamond finesse, West should cover with the king to promote his ◊10. The sight of the ◊K hitting the table can easily tempt declarer to have the following thoughts, 'Great, the king is onside. I can win this trick with the ace'. If declarer does win this trick, he will find it impossible to win more than two tricks with the diamond suit. The 3NT contract will be set one trick no matter how the missing diamonds are distributed between the two defenders.

Now let us suppose declarer resists temptation and plays a small diamond from dummy on this first diamond trick, thereby losing to the king. After winning whatever the defense returns, declarer can use the ◊4 to get to dummy and will end up taking five diamond tricks. This will result in his making 3NT with two overtricks. Entry problems often require declarer to lose an early round of a suit. Please remember to use your skill and resist the temptation of a Trojan horse.

Resisting temptation may also be an issue for the defense. If East started with Kxx in diamonds, he must not win the jack with the king. Even if East has Kx in diamonds it is not unreasonable to duck! Declarer will probably take a second finesse. If East ducks the first round smoothly with Kx and is allowed to win the second, he will have a great story.

The idea of duplicating hands goes back to the days of Whist. In the Winter of 1857, an argument took place at a dinner party over the relative importance of skill and luck at Whist. This led to the first duplicate team match. All duplicate bridge players have heard of the Mitchell and Howell movements for pairs events. These movements were originally designed for duplicate whist. Since Mitchell died in 1914 and Howell in 1907, clearly neither played our present form of bridge, which did not exist until 1925. They would both be shocked by their fame at a game neither of them ever played. If you are interested, the discussion of Problem 20 mentions two excellent books on the history of bridge.

After a good session most bridge players feel the game is more skill than luck. Of course, after a bad session it is more luck than skill!

**Type of play:** Entry management.

**Inspirational features:**
1) A long suit in dummy.
2) No entries to dummy outside of that long suit.

**Lose trick or do not try to win a trick:** Must resist the temptation to win West's ◊K with the ace.

**Create deal exercise:** Modify the deal so that dummy has both the ◊A and the ◊K.

**North**
- ♠ Q J 9 4
- ♡ A J 10 8 5
- ◇ 6 2
- ♣ A 4

**West**
- ♠ 7 3
- ♡ 9 7 4
- ◇ K Q 9 7 5
- ♣ K 9 8

Dealer W
Neither Vul.

**East**
- ♠ 6 5 2
- ♡ 6 3
- ◇ A J 10
- ♣ Q J 10 6 3

**South**
- ♠ A K 10 8
- ♡ K Q 2
- ◇ 8 4 3
- ♣ 7 5 2

| West | North | East | South |
|------|-------|------|-------|
| pass | 1♡ | pass | 1♠ |
| pass | 2♠ | pass | 4♡ |
| pass | 4♠ | all pass | |

Would you prefer to be declarer in 4♠ or 4♡ on this deal? Is there a general conclusion you can draw from your answer?

During the bidding, when partners are communicating to ascertain their combined assets, several questions are being answered. The most obvious and important question is, 'How many points do we have?' The second most important question is, 'Do we have an eight-card fit in either major?' Usually if a partnership holds eight or more cards in a major they would want to select it as the trump suit.

On the illustrated deal the North-South partnership has both an eight-card heart fit and an eight-card spade fit. Either suit would be a reasonable choice as the trump suit.

If the partnership is playing five-card majors, South can jump to 4♡ since he knows that their combined strength is enough for game and he knows they have a 5-3 heart fit. South expects but cannot be certain of a 4-4 spade fit since North may have raised spades with only three spades. North, however, is certain of the 4-4 spade fit and correctly bids 4♠ choosing to play in the 4-4 fit rather than the 5-3 fit. This is usually the better choice since the 5-3 fit in a side suit will often enable declarer to discard losers while a 4-4 fit in a side suit will not.

Suppose the defense starts by winning two rounds of diamonds and then shifts to a club. Declarer will win the club, pull trumps in three rounds, and run five heart tricks. On the fourth and fifth round of hearts declarer discards two clubs from his hand. After a club is ruffed in South and a diamond is ruffed in North, declarer winds up winning eleven tricks. If after pulling two rounds of trumps declarer discovers that the trump suit is breaking 4-1, he can still win eleven tricks by ruffing a diamond before pulling the remaining trumps in two rounds.

If North-South had stopped in the 4♡ contract, declarer would have lost a club trick in addition to the two diamond tricks. This would still have resulted in making the 4♡ contract but winning only ten tricks. That extra trick is important, particularly at duplicate bridge.

In general, if a partnership has both a 4-4 fit and a 5-3 fit in the majors, it is slightly more desirable to choose the 4-4 fit as the trump suit.

**Type of play:** Discards from a long suit.

**Inspirational feature:** This is the only problem in the book where the bidding is the main point. A side suit that has the same length in both declarer and dummy will not provide any discards in other suits. Therefore, it is usually more useful to have side suits of uneven length.

**Lose trick or do not try to win a trick:** −

**Create deal exercise:** Modify this deal so that a partnership has a 4-4 fit in one major and a 5-4 fit in the other major where playing in a 4-4 trump fit wins more tricks than a 5-4 trump fit.

**North**
- ♠ 8 2
- ♡ K 9 8 7
- ◊ J 7 6 4
- ♣ A Q 5

**West**
- ♠ Q J 10 9 7 6
- ♡ 6 4
- ◊ A 3
- ♣ 9 4 2

Dealer W
Neither Vul.

**East**
- ♠ 5 3
- ♡ Q J 3 2
- ◊ K 2
- ♣ J 10 8 6 3

**South**
- ♠ A K 4
- ♡ A 10 5
- ◊ Q 10 9 8 5
- ♣ K 7

| West | North | East | South |
|------|-------|------|-------|
| 2♠ | pass | pass | 2NT |
| pass | 3NT | all pass | |

West leads the ♠Q, of course. How do you intend to set up diamonds without allowing the defense to cash too many spade winners?

A hold-up play is a tactic by which a player refuses to win a trick in order to interfere with the opponents' communications. The best known situation in which to use a hold-up play occurs when the contract is notrump and declarer has only one stopper in the suit opened by the defenders. For example, declarer has Axx in his own hand opposite xx in dummy. When the defenders lead this suit, declarer will usually hold up two rounds and win the third round with the hope that if the suit is breaking 5-3, the defender with the five-card suit has no entry to his hand. If declarer is sure the suit is breaking 6-2 he can just as well win the second round played by the defenders.

If declarer has two stoppers, say AKx opposite xx, it is still often correct to hold up. Declarer can either hold up the first round or win the first round but then hold up on the second round. The illustrated deal demonstrates that there may be a big difference between these alternative ways of holding up.

Suppose declarer wins the spade lead and plays the ◊Q. East will win with the king and play a spade. On this trick declarer can hold up but West can overtake in order to gain the lead. This will enable West to continue with the ♠J, driving out declarer's last spade stopper.  Now if declarer tries to establish diamonds, West wins the ace and cashes three spade winners for down two.

Now suppose declarer holds up on the first round of spades and wins the second round.  If the ◊Q is led and East wins with the king, East will not have a spade to play.  Eventually declarer can safely drive out the ◊A since he still has a spade stopper.  Declarer will make 3NT with an overtrick.

Declarer's play of holding up on the first round was indicated by the 2♠ bid since West could be expected to have a six-card suit but probably, at most, one outside entry.

**A note about the defense:**  In the first case where declarer won the opening lead and played the ◊Q, it was essential for West to let East win the first round and play a spade.  If West wastes his entry on the first round of diamonds in order to get in and play spades, when East wins the second round of diamonds he will no longer have a spade to play back and declarer will make his contract.  In this case, even though declarer has misplayed the hand the defense has allowed the contract to be made – a not uncommon occurrence at the bridge table.

**Type of play:**  Hold up.  Sever communications.

**Inspirational features:**
1) The 2♠ bid gave declarer useful information about the split in the spade suit and the location of the outside strength.
2) South's spade holding enables declarer to hold up on the first or second round.
3) East can be prevented from playing a spade when East wins a diamond.

**Lose trick or do not try to win a trick:**  Hold up on the first trick.  The second trick is too late.

**Create deal exercise:**  Modify this deal so that West has only a five-card spade suit.

**North**
- ♠ 8 7 6
- ♡ A 4
- ◊ A J 10 4 3
- ♣ K 7 6

**West**
- ♠ K 9 4
- ♡ K J 10 9 5
- ◊ 8 6
- ♣ A 4 3

*Dealer W*
*Both Vul.*

**East**
- ♠ J 10 3 2
- ♡ 8 7 6 3
- ◊ 7 2
- ♣ Q J 2

**South**
- ♠ A Q 5
- ♡ Q 2
- ◊ K Q 9 5
- ♣ 10 9 8 5

| West | North | East | South |
|------|-------|------|-------|
| pass | 1◊ | pass | 3NT |
| all pass | | | |

West leads the ♡J, you play low from dummy, and your queen wins. First hurdle safely passed! How will you play from here?

In the game of Whist, the trump suit is determined by turning over the last card dealt. The suit of that card automatically becomes the trump suit. Obviously, there is no bidding. This saves players from arguments over bidding misunderstandings!

Just over 100 years ago whist players began converting to bridge. This first form of bridge involved a very primitive form of bidding and a dummy. The concept of a dummy was not entirely new to whist players who had played a 3-player form of their game called 'dummy whist'. The bidding in this first form of bridge was noncompetitive: only the dealer or his partner could name the trump suit (or notrump). Auction bridge, which did not exist until approximately 1907, introduced competitive bidding. Anyone interested in the history of bridge should read either *The Golden Age of Contract Bridge* by David Daniels (Scarborough Books, 1982) or *The Walk of the Oysters* by Rex Mackey (W.H. Allen, 1964). These books describe many theories on why the new game was called 'bridge'. While reading through old books on games I found that in the game of Euchre there is a bidding situation called 'at the bridge'; books written at that time simply called it 'bridge'. Since this situation has many similarities to the earliest form of bidding in bridge, it may have played a role in the naming of the new game 'bridge'.

The concept of a dummy may have seemed like a change that would simplify whist/bridge. In actuality the opposite is true since bridge players have more information which results in an increased importance of skill and a decreased importance of luck. At bridge, the only card played when the dummy is not visible is the opening lead. The leader has only his hand and the bidding as a guide. There is a great deal of luck involved in the success of the opening lead. Consider the illustrated deal where the opening lead of the ♡J is both good news and bad news for declarer. The good news is that declarer will win two heart tricks if West has led away from the ♡K. The bad news is that declarer is left with only one heart stopper.

With the help of the heart lead, declarer has eight top tricks and has two opportunities for a ninth trick: either with West holding the ♣A or East holding the ♠K. Which finesse should be taken? Both, if done in the proper order.

Suppose the spade finesse is taken first. After it loses to the king, West will play a second round of hearts leaving declarer without a heart stopper. Declarer would still need to find a ninth trick. Now it is impossible to play a club to the king since even if West holds the ace, West will win this trick and cash three hearts, setting declarer.

Now let's consider first playing a club to the king. Since in this example West has the ♣A this finesse succeeds, thereby providing declarer with a ninth trick. Let us now suppose that East held the ♣A. Then the ♣K would lose and East would play a second round of hearts. After winning the heart, even though declarer no longer has a heart stopper, he can still try the spade finesse for a ninth trick. This line of play will make 3NT if either finesse is successful. If neither finesse is successful declarer will go down several tricks but it is worth the risk to try to make 3NT.

With proper play declarer can take both finesses, not just one.

**Type of play:** Timing.

**Inspirational features:**
1) Fear of losing at least three heart tricks.
2) The club finesse cannot be taken if the spade finesse fails.
3) The spade finesse can still be taken if the club finesse fails.

**Lose trick or do not try to win a trick:** −

**Create deal exercise:** Modify this deal so that declarer has a potential finesse against the ♠Q.

Dealer: South
East-West vul.

**North**
- ♠  K 4 2
- ♡  8 6 3
- ◊  A 9 8 4
- ♣  8 7 5

**South**
- ♠  A Q J 10
- ♡  —
- ◊  7 5 3 2
- ♣  A K Q J 10

| West | North | East | South |
|------|-------|------|-------|
|      |       |      | 1♣ |
| pass | 1◊ | 1♡ | 1♠ |
| 2♡ | 2♠ | 3♡ | 4♠ |
| all pass | | | |

West leads the ♡4, and presents you with an immediate problem. Can you solve it?

Dealer: West
Neither vul.

**North**
- ♠  Q J 8
- ♡  10 8 5
- ◊  A K Q 2
- ♣  6 5 2

**South**
- ♠  A 4 2
- ♡  A K Q J 7
- ◊  5 3
- ♣  9 7 4

| West | North | East | South |
|------|-------|------|-------|
| 1◊ | pass | pass | 2♡ |
| pass | 4♡ | all pass | |

West leads the ♣A, and after taking the three top clubs, exits with a heart. The spade finesse doesn't look like a very good bet – but do you have any other options?

## PROBLEM 23  A LARGE BLIND SPOT

Dealer: East
East-West vul.

**North**
♠ A Q 9 5
♡ J 10 8
◇ 7 4 3
♣ A J 9

**South**
♠ K J 10 4 2
♡ —
◇ 10 9 8
♣ K Q 10 8 7

| West | North | East | South |
|------|-------|------|-------|
|      |       | 1♡   | 1♠    |
| 2♡   | 3♡¹   | 4♡   | 4♠    |
| pass | pass  | 5♡   | 5♠    |
| all pass |    |      |       |

West leads the ♡3 — not unexpected, and allowing you to escape three quick diamond losers. Eleven tricks are easy — can you see a way to take more?

## PROBLEM 24  OVERBIDDING SOMETIMES PAYS OFF

Dealer: South
East-West vul.

**North**
♠ Q J 10 6 5
♡ K Q J 10 5
◇ —
♣ Q J 10

**South**
♠ A K 9 8 7
♡ —
◇ 8 6 5 3 2
♣ A K 3

| West | North | East | South |
|------|-------|------|-------|
|      |       |      | 1♠    |
| pass | 4◇¹   | dbl  | 4♡    |
| pass | 4♠    | pass | 5♣    |
| pass | 5◇    | pass | 7♠    |
| all pass |   |      |       |

1. Splinter bid.

West leads the ◇4. How will you make thirteen tricks?

**North**
- ♠ K 4 2
- ♡ 8 6 3
- ◇ A 9 8 4
- ♣ 8 7 5

**West**
- ♠ 9 8 5 3
- ♡ Q 9 7 4
- ◇ K J 10
- ♣ 9 6

*Dealer S*
*EW Vul.*

**East**
- ♠ 7 6
- ♡ A K J 10 5 2
- ◇ Q 6
- ♣ 4 3 2

**South**
- ♠ A Q J 10
- ♡ —
- ◇ 7 5 3 2
- ♣ A K Q J 10

| West | North | East | South |
|------|-------|------|-------|
|  |  |  | 1♣ |
| pass | 1◇ | 1♡ | 1♠ |
| 2♡ | 2♠ | 3♡ | 4♠ |
| all pass |  |  |  |

West leads the ♡4, and presents you with an immediate problem. Can you solve it?

If a present day bridge player were to glance at a bridge book on declarer play from the 1930's he would feel right at home. The great classic *Watson on the Play of the Hand (1934)* is still widely read for its content by modern bridge players. This does not carry over to books that discuss bridge bidding, since bidding systems are continually evolving. In the 1950's and 1960's the style of the Goren System was to open a four-card major and raise partner with Qxx or better. This often led to declarer playing in a 4-3 trump fit. Modern bidding systems reduce the frequency in which declarer finds himself playing in a 4-3 trump fit. Declarers in the 1960's were probably better than modern declarers at handling these trump fits since they had such extensive experience. Alphonse (Sonny) Moyse Jr. (1898-1973) encouraged playing in 4-3 fits and had a reputation for such excellent declarer play in these contracts that a 4-3 trump fit is referred to as a Moysian fit.

Consider the illustrated deal where modern bridge players may end up in a Moysian fit.

With the heart void, declarer might be tempted to ruff the opening heart lead. Unless the defenders' six trump cards break 3-3, this would be a mistake. If declarer pulls three rounds of spades after ruffing the lead, he will find himself out of trumps while the defenders still have a trump and a running heart suit. Declarer will go down several tricks. Declarer does not have to try to pull all of defenders' trump cards after ruffing the opening lead, but other lines are also doomed. In order to discern the best line of play we must consider the likelihood of different trump distributions in the defenders' hands. When the defenders hold six trump cards, the chance of the defenders' trumps breaking 3-3 is 36% and the chance of their breaking 4-2 is 48%. Therefore if declarer can play four rounds of spades he has an 84% chance of pulling all the defenders' trumps. Clearly declarer's top priority must be to protect his four-card trump suit so that he has the ability to play four rounds of spades.

On the opening trick declarer should not diminish his trump holding by ruffing but should instead throw a diamond. If the defense continues with a heart on the second trick, declarer should throw a second diamond. If a third heart is played, throw a third diamond. If a fourth heart is played, *ruff in dummy with the king, not in your hand;* you are still protecting your four trumps. Now you can draw trumps successfully in four rounds and claim the rest of the tricks.

Notice that you lost nothing by refusing to ruff the hearts since even if you ruffed the first trick and were fortunate enough to get a 3-3 trump break, you would still only win ten tricks. Why gamble if there is nothing to gain?

**Type of play:** Trump management.

**Inspirational features:**
1) Fear of being forced to trump in the long trump hand while possessing only a seven-card trump fit (particularly a 4-3 fit).
2) Three slow diamond losers.

**Lose trick or do not try to win a trick:** Three times, declarer must resist ruffing a heart.

**Create deal exercise:** Modify this deal so that declarer has a 5-2 trump fit where he must protect his trump holding.

**North**
- ♠ Q J 8
- ♡ 10 8 5
- ◊ A K Q 2
- ♣ 6 5 2

**West**
- ♠ K 7 3
- ♡ 6 4 3
- ◊ J 10 9 8
- ♣ A K Q

*Dealer W*
*Neither Vul.*

**East**
- ♠ 10 9 6 5
- ♡ 9 2
- ◊ 7 6 4
- ♣ J 10 8 3

**South**
- ♠ A 4 2
- ♡ A K Q J 7
- ◊ 5 3
- ♣ 9 7 4

| West | North | East | South |
|------|-------|------|-------|
| 1◊ | pass | pass | 2♡ |
| pass | 4♡ | all pass | |

West leads the ♣A, and after taking the three top clubs, exits with a heart. The spade finesse doesn't look like a very good bet — but do you have any other option?

When the opponents' bidding has stopped at a low level and the last two players have passed, a bridge player is in what is called the balancing seat. Obviously a pass in this position will end the bidding. A bid made in the balancing seat may describe a different hand from the same bid when one is in the direct seat. On the illustrated deal, South overcalled 2♡ in the balancing seat. North correctly realized that South's jump overcall was not weak but showed a full opener and bid 4♡.

West took three club tricks and switched to the ♡3. Now declarer has nine top tricks: five hearts, three diamonds, and a spade. In order to find a tenth trick declarer might be tempted to take a spade finesse. However, since the defense only has 14 HCP, West pretty much has to hold the ♠K as he opened the bidding. West must also have at least four diamonds since he bid 1◊ rather than 1♣ while holding the ace, king, and queen of clubs. Proper use of this information will guarantee the success of this contract. Declarer knows West cannot discard the ♠K, or the ♠Q will become the tenth trick. Likewise, West must keep four diamonds, or the ◊2 in dummy will represent the tenth trick for declarer.

After winning the fourth trick, declarer should cash the ♠A and the other four heart winners. This is the ending when the last heart is led.

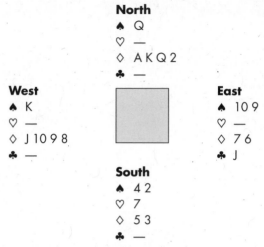

**North**
♠ Q
♡ —
◇ A K Q 2
♣ —

**West**
♠ K
♡ —
◇ J 10 9 8
♣ —

**East**
♠ 10 9
♡ —
◇ 7 6
♣ J

**South**
♠ 4 2
♡ 7
◇ 5 3
♣ —

If West discards his ♠K, dummy will discard the ◇2. If West discards a diamond, dummy will discard the ♠Q. In either case, the last four tricks will be won in dummy. On this hand, it was essential to cash all five trump tricks in order to create this impossible situation for West.

Without the information from the bidding, declarer should take the spade finesse (50% chance) rather than try for the squeeze. The squeeze play succeeds only when West has the ♠K and four or more diamonds (slightly less than a 25% chance). When you become declarer, recall the bidding of your opponents. Often they have inadvertently become your helpers and told you how to play the hand.

**Type of play:** Simple squeeze. Card reading.

**Inspirational features:**
1) Declarer has two threat cards for a squeeze: the ◇2 and the ♠Q. My book on simple squeezes labels them **strong threat cards** since only one defender can prevent them from winning a trick.
2) West's 1◇ bid indicates that he can be overworked with the two jobs of preventing both threat cards from winning a trick.
3) After the defense takes three club tricks, declarer has nine top cards for the last ten tricks.

**Lose trick or do not try to win a trick:** —

**Create deal exercise:** Modify this deal so that declarer has a spade threat card in the South hand instead of the North hand.

**North**
- ♠ A Q 9 5
- ♡ J 10 8
- ◊ 7 4 3
- ♣ A J 9

**West**
- ♠ 7 6 3
- ♡ 7 6 5 3
- ◊ K J 5
- ♣ 4 3 2

Dealer E
EW Vul.

**East**
- ♠ 8
- ♡ A K Q 9 4 2
- ◊ A Q 6 2
- ♣ 6 5

**South**
- ♠ K J 10 4 2
- ♡ —
- ◊ 10 9 8
- ♣ K Q 10 8 7

| West | North | East | South |
|------|-------|------|-------|
|      |       | 1♡   | 1♠    |
| 2♡   | 3♡    | 4♡   | 4♠    |
| pass | pass  | 5♡   | 5♠    |
| all pass |   |      |       |

West leads the ♡3 – not unexpected, and allowing you to escape three quick diamond losers. Eleven tricks are easy – but can you see a way to take more?

After West squeezed out a 2♡ bid based on four-card trump support, the 3♡ cuebid by North showed spade support with at least 10 points. Both sides have a double fit which enables North-South to make 4♠ against any defense, and East-West to make 4♡ against any defense.

On the illustrated deal, declarer was overjoyed by the heart lead since the defenders missed an opportunity to take three quick diamond tricks, which would have set the contract. The heart lead enables declarer to ruff the heart lead, draw trumps in three rounds, run five club winners (discarding two diamonds in dummy) and to eventually ruff a diamond with the remaining trump in dummy. Declarer won eleven tricks (six trump tricks and five club tricks).

However, declarer had a blind spot – he missed a line of play that would have produced twelve tricks. After the heart lead, declarer had the perfect hand for what is called a **dummy reversal.** Declarer can ruff the heart lead, play one round of trumps winning in dummy, ruff a second heart, play a second round of trumps again winning in dummy, ruff the third heart, enter dummy with a club, and pull the last trump. This line of play will result in winning twelve tricks (seven trump tricks and five club tricks).

The blind spot that declarer had on this hand was the result of habit and experience. In almost all trump contracts declarer is trying to ruff in the hand that has the shorter trump suit. With a dummy reversal, however, one deviates from this habit by ruffing in the hand that has the longer trump suit and eventually pulling trumps with the hand that originally had the shorter trump suit.

When playing duplicate bridge the extra trick is very important. Actually duplicate was almost given a different name in the nineteenth century. In 1894, R. F. Foster authored *Duplicate Whist and Whist Strategy*. He objected to the name *duplicate* since tournament play involved passing the boards containing the deals from table to table. Similar to most club games, the cards are dealt once and then played over and over. The hands are never actually duplicated. He recommended renaming duplicate whist, *overplay whist* or *Rejoué*. Even though we don't usually 'duplicate' boards in most one-section club games, too much time of a bridge player's life is spent duplicating boards at Regionals and Sectionals. The present name is certainly appropriate.

**Type of play:** Dummy reversal.

**Inspirational features:**
1) The ability to ruff several cards in the long trump hand; eventually the long trump hand will actually become the short trump hand.
2) Enough top trump cards in the short trump hand to look after the defenders' spades.
3) Enough entries to the short trump hand.

**Lose trick or do not try to win a trick:** –

Note: Compare this deal to Problem 21. In that example, declarer can ruff three hearts but does not have top trump cards in dummy to pull the defenders' trumps.

**Create deal exercise:** Modify this deal so that South has six trump cards and North has three trump cards.

**North**
- ♠ Q J 10 6 5
- ♡ K Q J 10 5
- ◇ —
- ♣ Q J 10

**West**
- ♠ 4
- ♡ A 9 8 3 2
- ◇ Q 9 4
- ♣ 9 8 7 4

*Dealer S*
*EW Vul.*

**East**
- ♠ 3 2
- ♡ 7 6 4
- ◇ A K J 10 7
- ♣ 6 5 2

**South**
- ♠ A K 9 8 7
- ♡ —
- ◇ 8 6 5 3 2
- ♣ A K 3

| West | North | East | South |
|------|-------|------|-------|
| | | | 1♠ |
| pass | 4◇¹ | dbl | 4♡ |
| pass | 4♠ | pass | 5♣ |
| pass | 5◇ | pass | 7♠ |
| all pass | | | |

1. Splinter bid.

West leads the ◇4. How will you make thirteen tricks?

Splinter bids are a powerful weapon in the arsenal of bridge players. They allow a partnership to detect an excellent distributional fit, which at times enables them to bid small slams with barely enough high card points to bid game.

   North's double jump to 4◇ was a splinter bid. It indicated a singleton or void in diamonds, at least four spades, and approximately the values of a minimum opening hand. After the splinter bid, South can assess the value of North's diamond shortness. For example, if South were to hold the ace and king in diamonds instead of in clubs, North's shortness and ruffing ability would be useless. On this hand, South can see great value in North's shortness since South has no wasted high cards in diamonds.

   As spades was the agreed trump suit, South's bids of 4♡ and 5♣ were **cuebids** showing first-round controls. North's 5◇ cuebid showed first-round control of diamonds. South was in a frisky mood and jumped to 7♠. A more prudent bidder would have been content just to reach 6♠.

When dummy hit the table, South could now admire the excellent fit. Thirteen tricks can be won if declarer is able to win three club tricks and crossruff the hand to win ten tricks with trumps. During the crossruff of diamonds and hearts, declarer does not have to concern himself with the distribution of the East-West cards in these suits; the defense cannot overruff because he is crossruffing with top trumps.

The interesting point on this deal is that declarer must cash all three club tricks before starting the crossruff. Otherwise, during the crossruff East-West will discard their small clubs, and eventually when declarer plays clubs, the defense will be able to ruff his winners. Some declarers are afraid to play clubs before the crossruff for fear that the defense might ruff one of the three club tricks. It is true that allowing the defense to ruff a winning trick is a bit embarrassing when you hold the top ten cards in the trump suit. Declarer, however, has no choice but to gamble that the East-West club suit will break 4-3 (a 62% chance). If he delays playing clubs until the defenders have an opportunity to discard clubs during the crossruff, he can be certain they will ruff a club winner. As a general principle, on crossruff hands where trumps are never drawn, it is necessary to cash your outside winners before attempting the crossruff.

Of course if the defense had led a trump, declarer would have been set since he would have only won nine trump tricks and three club tricks. However, after East's lead-directing double, West was likely to lead a diamond.

The word *slam* was the name of a game that was a predecessor of both whist and bridge. It dates back to the 1600s. Sometimes it was spelled *slamm*. A slam at whist meant winning all thirteen tricks. Starting around 1890 an extra reward was given for winning twelve tricks and the present distinction was created between a grand and small slam. Originally a small slam was called a little slam. Many sports such as tennis and golf have stolen our term 'grand slam' for winning everything.

**Type of play:** Crossruff.

**Inspirational features:**
1) Long trumps in both declarer's hand and dummy.
2) Shortness in different side suits.
3) Lack of a side suit that can be established.
4) Realizing that when the defenders cannot follow suit and cannot overruff, they will discard clubs and later ruff your club winners.

**Lose trick or do not try to win a trick:** —

**Create deal exercise:** Modify this deal so that declarer should play one round of trumps before playing clubs.

Dealer: East
North-South vul.

**North**
♠ K 6
♡ A 5
◇ A 10 9 8 6
♣ A J 10 7

**South**
♠ A 5 3
♡ K 6 2
◇ K 7 5
♣ K Q 9 5

| West | North | East | South |
|------|-------|------|-------|
|      |       | pass | 1NT   |
| pass | 6NT   | all pass |   |

West leads the ♡Q. Clearly you will need four diamond tricks – how do you plan to get them?

Dealer: West
Both vul.

**North**
♠ Q 10 3
♡ 7 2
◇ Q J 9 5
♣ A Q 10 8

**South**
♠ A K J 8
♡ J 10 5
◇ A K 4
♣ 7 6 2

| West | North | East | South |
|------|-------|------|-------|
| pass | pass  | pass | 1NT   |
| pass | 3NT   | all pass |   |

West leads the ♣5. At many forms of the game, you will simply take your nine top tricks here and get on with the next deal. But you are playing matchpoints — should you try for overtricks, and if so, how?

## PROBLEM 27   ARE YOU A WINNER OR A LOSER?

Dealer: East
East-West vul.

**North**
- ♠ 10 9 8 3
- ♡ Q 3
- ◊ A K 7 6 2
- ♣ K 4

**South**
- ♠ A K Q J 4 2
- ♡ 5
- ◊ 5 4 3
- ♣ 10 6 2

| West | North | East | South |
|------|-------|------|-------|
|      |       | 1♡   | 1♠    |
| 2♡   | 3♡    | 4♡   | 4♠    |
| all pass |   |      |       |

West leads the ♡2. It's a pretty good bet that East has the ♣A, so playing a club to the king is unlikely to work. Do you see any alternative?

## PROBLEM 28   DON'T REGRET THE CORRECT PLAY

Dealer: East
Neither vul.

**North**
- ♠ A 6
- ♡ Q J 7 4
- ◊ J 7 5 2
- ♣ K Q 8

**South**
- ♠ K Q 10 9 7 3
- ♡ A K 5
- ◊ 8
- ♣ A 10 2

| West | North | East | South |
|------|-------|------|-------|
|      |       | pass | 1♠    |
| pass | 2NT   | pass | 4♣    |
| pass | 4♡    | pass | 6♠    |
| all pass |   |      |       |

West starts with the ◊K, and you ruff the second round of diamonds. Now
you play the ♠A followed by the ♠K, but West discards the ◊3 on this trick.
Unlucky. Do you have any chance left to make the hand?

**North**
♠ K 6
♡ A 5
◇ A 10 9 8 6
♣ A J 10 7

**West**
♠ J 9 8 2
♡ Q J 10 7
◇ Q J 4 2
♣ 6

Dealer E
NS Vul.

**East**
♠ Q 10 7 4
♡ 9 8 4 3
◇ 3
♣ 8 4 3 2

**South**
♠ A 5 3
♡ K 6 2
◇ K 7 5
♣ K Q 9 5

| West | North | East | South |
|------|-------|------|-------|
|      |       | pass | 1NT |
| pass | 6NT | all pass | |

West leads the ♡Q. Clearly you will need four diamond tricks — how do you plan to get them?

A **safety play** occurs when declarer chooses to play a suit in a fashion that will protect him against a bad break in that suit. Usually this implies that declarer is willing to sacrifice overtricks in order to increase the likelihood that the contract is successful. In some bridge books, the author's definition of a safety play *requires* that potential overtricks be risked. These authors feel that without the risk it is just a case of applying proper technique to the play of a suit and should not be called a safety play. Other authors use the more general definition.

Recent bridge books devote less space to safety plays than older ones since today the most common form of tournament bridge is matchpoint duplicate pairs, where the scoring method places a great value on overtricks. Often declarer will be willing to risk a contract in order to increase his chance of overtricks. This may be the proper decision for this method of scoring but it clearly diminishes the appeal of many safety plays.

On the illustrated deal, declarer must win four diamond tricks in order to make the 6NT contract. Simply playing the ace and the king on the first two diamond tricks will be successful whenever the diamond suit breaks 3-2. There is a 68% chance this will occur. Declarer will also be successful when the suit breaks 4-1 and the singleton is the jack or queen. There is an 11% chance this will occur. Therefore declarer will be successful almost 80% of the time with this line of play. But before he gets elated with his likely success, he should consider whether he can protect himself from other 4-1 breaks and even 5-0 breaks.

Declarer should try to figure out which defender is most likely to have four or five diamonds. By playing two rounds of clubs, he will learn that West started with only one club. Thus West is more likely than East to have four or five diamonds. Based on this information, declarer can win the first round of diamonds with the king. On the second round of diamonds, he can play a small diamond out of his hand. If West does not play an honor, declarer should play a small diamond from dummy. If East has either diamond honor this trick will be lost, but then the ace will win the third trick and drop the other diamond honor. On the illustrated deal, declarer will win the second trick, and the ◊A will win the third while capturing a diamond honor. After the defense wins the fourth round of diamonds, the remaining diamond in dummy will be declarer's twelfth trick. Even if East had shown out of diamonds on the first round, declarer could finesse West's honors twice and still take four diamond tricks.

Playing two rounds of clubs is called a **discovery play** since its purpose was to obtain information that would help declarer decide how to play the diamond suit. If, when declarer played the two rounds of clubs, he had learned that East rather than West had started with only one club, he should assume East had long diamonds. If clubs had broken 3-2, it would have been harder to judge which defender was more likely to have long diamonds.

Even though bridge experts may disagree on whether this is an example of a safety play, they will agree that it is essential to anticipate and prepare for bad breaks. One advantage of bridge over athletic sports is that when players say they had a bad break, they are referring to a suit and not a bone!

**Type of play:** Safety play. Discovery play. Counting of one suit.

**Inspirational features:**
1) Fear of two losers in the suit.
2) Count of the club suit can aid declarer when playing the diamond suit.

**Lose trick or do not try to win a trick:** Lose a diamond trick that could be won to decrease the chance of losing two tricks in the suit.

**Create deal exercise:** Modify this deal so that both North and South have four diamonds.

**North**
♠ Q 10 3
♡ 7 2
♦ Q J 9 5
♣ A Q 10 8

**West**
♠ 9 4 2
♡ K 6 3
♦ 8 6
♣ K J 9 5 3

*Dealer W*
*Both Vul.*

**East**
♠ 7 6 5
♡ A Q 9 8 4
♦ 10 7 3 2
♣ 4

**South**
♠ A K J 8
♡ J 10 5
♦ A K 4
♣ 7 6 2

| West | North | East | South |
|------|-------|------|-------|
| pass | pass | pass | 1NT |
| pass | 3NT | all pass | |

West leads the ♣5. At many forms of the game, you will simply take your nine top tricks here and get on with the next deal. But you are playing matchpoints — should you try for overtricks, and if so, how?

One of the first maxims a new bridge player learns is 'When defending against NT, lead the fourth highest card of a long suit'. The main goal of this principle is to try to develop tricks in that long suit. Leading fourth best also enables the partner of the opening leader to determine how many cards declarer holds in the led suit that are higher than the spot card led. This information may help the defense. It is obtained by applying the Rule of Eleven, which is described by the following steps:
1) Subtract the number on the spot card led from eleven.
2) Count the cards you hold in that suit higher than the card led.
3) Count the cards dummy holds in the suit higher than the card led.
4) Add the results of Step 2 and Step 3.
5) Subtract the result of Step 4 from Step 1. This value represents the number of cards declarer holds higher than the spot card led.

On the illustrated deal, declarer can easily take the nine tricks required of 3NT: one club trick, four spade tricks, and four diamond tricks. Clearly declarer cannot afford to lose a trick in the club suit since the defense would be able to grab enough heart tricks to set the contract. However, in duplicate pairs, there are substantial rewards for overtricks, so there is some temptation for declarer to gamble and try to win the first club trick with the ♣Q, or even the ♣10, or for that matter the ♣8. What to do?

The answer is revealed by the lead of the ♣5. Since there is nothing in the bidding that would encourage West to lead from a short minor suit, it is reasonable to assume that West is leading fourth best from a long club suit. Now declarer can steal information by applying the same Rule of Eleven that was intended to help East with the defense. In effect, declarer can decode enemy information. Declarer need simply follow steps 1 through 4 and realize that the value obtained in Step 5 will represent the number of cards East holds higher than the spot card led. For this example, the five steps are:

1) 11-5=6    2) 2    3) 4    4) 2+4=6    5) 6-6=0

Now declarer knows that East cannot have any club cards higher than the ♣5. Therefore he can safely win the first trick with the ♣8. Assuming West led fourth best, this deep finesse is guaranteed by the Rule of Eleven. Declarer will return to his hand twice in order to take two more finesses in the club suit. As a result, declarer will take twelve tricks while the defenders are thinking about how much they would have enjoyed cashing their five heart tricks. Fortunately, at the time of the opening lead, West had no way of knowing about the beautiful heart suit held by East.

Do not try to memorize this five-step recipe. It was only a convenient method for describing the Rule of Eleven. Players only need to appreciate that the result of Step 1 is the total number of cards higher than the opening lead in the three hands other than the leader's. The Rule of Eleven works equally well in a suit contract if the defenders lead fourth best. Of course, if an opening leader makes an unorthodox lead, you may feel foolish, and worse still look foolish, with your deep finesse when the Rule leads you astray. Don't be a chicken. Bridge is only a game.

**Type of play:**  Rule of Eleven.

**Inspirational features:**
1) Desire to peek at East's club cards in order to discover the lowest card in dummy that will definitely win the first trick.
2) The defense could win enough heart tricks to set declarer if he were to lose a club.

**Lose trick or do not try to win a trick:** —

**Create deal exercise:**  Modify this deal so that the ♣5 is in dummy and declarer is certain that it will win the first trick if West's opening lead is fourth best.

**North**
- ♠ 10 9 8 3
- ♡ Q 3
- ◇ A K 7 6 2
- ♣ K 4

**West**
- ♠ 7
- ♡ J 8 7 2
- ◇ Q J 10
- ♣ J 9 8 7 5

Dealer E
EW Vul.

**East**
- ♠ 6 5
- ♡ A K 10 9 6 4
- ◇ 9 8
- ♣ A Q 3

**South**
- ♠ A K Q J 4 2
- ♡ 5
- ◇ 5 4 3
- ♣ 10 6 2

| West | North | East | South |
|------|-------|------|-------|
|      |       | 1♡   | 1♠    |
| 2♡   | 3♡    | 4♡   | 4♠    |
| all pass |   |      |       |

West leads the ♡2. It's a pretty good bet that East has the ♣A, so playing a club to the king is unlikely to produce your tenth trick. Do you see any alternative?

Experienced bridge players often rely on a cuebid in an opponent's suit to describe their hands. The meaning of a cuebid is determined by the preceding auction. On the illustrated deal the 3♡ cuebid by North described a hand with at least three spades and 10 or more points. If East passes after the cuebid, South must bid 3♠ even with a minimum hand. The advantage of attaching this meaning to the cuebid is that it allows North to describe three different hands by having three ways to show a spade fit below the game level: 2♠, 3♠, or 3♡. Now both 2♠ and 3♠ indicate fewer than 10 points, but 3♠ would guarantee at least four-card trump support and usually shortness in a side suit.

On the illustrated deal the first trick was won by East's king. When the ♡A was led at Trick 2, declarer ruffed. Declarer could count either three or four losers: one heart, one diamond, and one or two clubs depending on which defender holds the ♣A. East's 1♡ bid meant that the ♣A was probably held by East, so South tried to avoid having the success of the contract depend on the club finesse by attempting to discard clubs on diamonds. He played two rounds of spades, and then played the ♢A, ♢K and ♢2. Declarer hoped diamonds would break 3-2 and that East would win the third round. After all, if East were to lead a club there would be only one club loser. Unfortunately the third round of diamonds was lost to West. West's obvious club return defeated the contract.

Declarer should not ruff the ♡A at Trick 2 but, instead, should discard the ♢3. This example of a loser-on-loser play will virtually guarantee the contract if diamonds break 3-2. On the third trick East will lead either a trump or a diamond. In either case declarer can draw trumps, cash the ♢A and ♢K, and ruff the ♢2. He can then return to dummy with a trump and cash two winning diamonds while discarding two clubs from the South hand. Declarer is left with only one club loser.

This loser-on-loser play virtually enables declarer to lose a diamond trick without allowing West to lead a club. This allows South the necessary time to establish the two additional diamond winners in dummy and discard two clubs.

Even if East had not led the ♡A at Trick 2, declarer could still employ this loser-on-loser play by entering dummy and leading the ♡Q. Since the purpose of this particular loser-on-loser play is to prevent West from being on lead it is an example of an **avoidance play.**

It is interesting to compare this problem to Problem 13 where a similar diamond suit is established when declarer must avoid losing a diamond.

Loser-on-loser plays are used for many different purposes but a declarer who recognizes them is clearly a winner.

**Type of play:** Loser-on-loser. Avoidance play. Establish a long suit.

**Inspirational features:**
1) The ♣K held by dummy makes it desirable to have East on lead rather than West.
2) Possessing a 5-3 fit in a side suit where the third round is a loser.
3) Slow loser in diamonds.

**Lose trick or do not try to win a trick:** Discard a diamond on a trick that could have been won with a ruff.

**Create deal exercise:** Modify this deal so that North only has a four-card diamond suit.

**North**
- ♠ A 6
- ♡ Q J 7 4
- ◇ J 7 5 2
- ♣ K Q 8

**West**
- ♠ 5
- ♡ 9 8 3
- ◇ K Q 9 4 3
- ♣ J 7 6 4

*Dealer E*
*Neither Vul.*

**East**
- ♠ J 8 4 2
- ♡ 10 6 2
- ◇ A 10 6
- ♣ 9 5 3

**South**
- ♠ K Q 10 9 7 3
- ♡ A K 5
- ◇ 8
- ♣ A 10 2

| West | North | East | South |
|------|-------|------|-------|
| | | pass | 1♠ |
| pass | 2NT | pass | 4♣ |
| pass | 4♡ | pass | 6♠ |
| all pass | | | |

West starts with the ◇K, and you ruff the second round of diamonds. Now you play the ♠A followed by the ♠K, but West discards the ◇3 on this trick. Unlucky. Do you have any chance left to make the hand?

Some readers might feel that Gerber 4♣ is an unnecessary convention since one could use Blackwood to ask about aces. However, on this deal a bid of 4NT by South after 2NT should not be Blackwood but rather a non-forcing invitation to 6NT (this is called a *quantitative* 4NT).

After declarer lost the first trick, he ruffed the ◇A on the second trick, won the third trick with the ♠A and won the fourth trick with the ♠K. When West discarded the ◇3 on the second round of trump, declarer regretted that he had not chosen to finesse the ♠10 instead of playing the king. Declarer should not have been annoyed at his decision since he had chosen the proper play, even though it worked out unfortunately. Since the probability that the trump suit would break 3-2 is 68%, declarer should try to pull trumps by playing three rounds of top spades rather than finessing. If declarer had finessed on this hand the defenders would have thought that he was either a poor bridge player or a cheater who had peeked at their cards.

Declarer should not waste his mental energy being upset over the trump situation but rather focus on a line of play to avoid what looks like a certain trump loser. The essence of the problem is that declarer would now like to take a trump finesse against East but no longer has a trump in dummy for this purpose. However, declarer can virtually finesse East's trump holding if he visualizes the following situation that he would want at the twelfth trick of the hand. South has the Q10 of trumps, East has the J8 of trumps, and the lead is in dummy. Whatever card is led from dummy, declarer will win the final two tricks. Declarer can achieve this ending by winning the fifth trick with the ♣K, ruffing the ◊7, cashing the ♣AQ, and then the three top hearts finishing with the queen. Now the two-trick ending with the lead in dummy, described above, is achieved and 6♠ will be made.

This deal is an example of a **trump coup.** A combination of both skill and luck was required on the hand. Skill was needed to visualize the two-trick ending and to appreciate the necessity of the diamond ruff in order to shorten declarer's trump holding so that it is the same length as East's trump holding. Without this, it would have been impossible to set up the ending required for a trump coup. If a diamond had not been led by the defenders on the second trick it would have been necessary for declarer to ruff diamonds twice in order to shorten his trump holding to the same length as East's. Declarer also needed some luck. If East did not have at least three cards in both clubs and hearts, the final ending could not have been achieved since East would be able to ruff the third round of clubs or hearts.

On some hands it might be necessary to trump winners in order to shorten your trumps and create the end situation required for a trump coup. When this rare play occurs it is called a **grand coup.**

One key to life, as well as to this deal, is the philosophy that when a bad situation occurs don't waste energy regretting what has occurred but search for a solution. If I could only follow my own advice!

**Type of play:** Trump Coup.

**Inspirational features:**
1) A need to finesse East in the trump suit but North lacks a spade to lead.
2) Many entries to North so that South can shorten his trumps to the same length as East.

**Lose trick or do not try to win a trick:** –

**Create deal exercise:** Modify this deal so that South executes a grand coup.

Dealer: East
Both vul.

**North**
♠ 7 6 3 2
♡ A K
◇ J 4 3
♣ A 7 6 3

**South**
♠ A K
♡ 8 6 4 2
◇ Q 10 9 8 5
♣ K 4

| West | North | East | South |
|------|-------|------|-------|
|  |  | pass | 1◇ |
| pass | 1♠ | pass | 1NT |
| pass | 3NT | all pass | |

West leads the ♠Q. Plan the play.

Dealer: East
Neither vul.

**North**
♠ J 9 8 5
♡ 8
◇ Q 10 9 8 5
♣ A K Q

**South**
♠ 10 7
♡ A K Q J
◇ J 7
♣ J 10 9 4 2

| West | North | East | South |
|------|-------|------|-------|
|  |  | pass | 1♣ |
| pass | 1◇ | pass | 1♡ |
| pass | 1♠ | pass | 1NT |
| pass | 3NT | all pass | |

West leads the ♡3 (phew!). You have nine winners, but the entry situation makes it difficult to enjoy them. Can you see any way to disentangle the situation?

Dealer: West
Both vul.

**North**
♠ 6 4
♡ K Q J
♢ K Q J 8
♣ A 7 6 4

**South**
♠ A Q 7 5 3 2
♡ 5 3
♢ 9 6
♣ K Q 2

| West | North | East | South |
|------|-------|------|-------|
| 1♡ | 1NT | pass | 4♠ |
| all pass | | | |

West leads the ♣J. There is no way to avoid losing the two red aces, so you have to hold your trump losers to one. How will you do that?

Dealer: North
Both vul.

**North**
♠ Q 8 6 4 2
♡ 10 6 4
♢ A J 10
♣ 6 4

**South**
♠ A K 9 5 3
♡ 7 5
♢ 8 7 2
♣ A K 5

| West | North | East | South |
|------|-------|------|-------|
| | pass | pass | 1♠ |
| dbl | 4♠ | all pass | |

West leads the ♡A, and continues the suit. You ruff the third round. How do plan to play diamonds to be certain to avoid two losers?

**North**
- ♠ 7 6 3 2
- ♡ A K
- ◇ J 4 3 .
- ♣ A 7 6 3

**West**
- ♠ Q J 10 9 8
- ♡ 9 7 3
- ◇ A 6
- ♣ 10 5 2

*Dealer E*
*Both Vul.*

**East**
- ♠ 5 4
- ♡ Q J 10 5
- ◇ K 7 2
- ♣ Q J 9 8

**South**
- ♠ A K
- ♡ 8 6 4 2
- ◇ Q 10 9 8 5
- ♣ K 4

| West | North | East | South |
|------|-------|------|-------|
|  |  | pass | 1◇ |
| pass | 1♠ | pass | 1NT |
| pass | 3NT | all pass |  |

West leads the ♠Q. Plan the play.

The blood pressure of a bridge player is probably the highest when he has to make an opening lead. This is the only time a card is played when the dummy is not visible, and the player must base his decision on only his own hand and the bidding. Very often the leader wishes he did not have to lead since there is a justifiable fear that a trick will be surrendered.

There are, however, several situations when a bridge player is happy to make an opening lead. A common situation arises when the defense is trying to develop tricks in their long suit before declarer can develop tricks in his long suit. The illustrated deal is an example of this situation. The defense is trying to develop spade tricks before declarer can develop his diamond tricks, so West is glad to strike first with the opening lead. If West has five spades and both the ◇A and the ◇K, South is doomed, but West would surely have overcalled with that holding.

When declarer sees the dummy he will consider the likely distributions of the East-West cards that will allow him to succeed in his contract. One possibility would be spades breaking 4-3. In this case, the defense can only take four tricks: the ◇A, the ◇K and two spade tricks. Another possibility would be that spades break 5-2 with East holding both the

$\Diamond A$ and the $\Diamond K$. In this situation East will be unable to get West on lead to cash the three spade winners. Since declarer will succeed in these cases no matter how he plays the diamond suit, he can now consider distributions of the East-West cards where the defense can set him only if they make the right decisions. Declarer should consider how to make these decisions as difficult as possible for the defense.

On the illustrated deal the spades break 5-2, and the diamond honors are split between East-West. Declarer would like to lose a round of diamonds to West before losing a diamond to East, so that when East gets in with the $\Diamond K$ he will no longer have a spade to play to his partner. In an attempt to achieve this, on the second trick declarer should play a low club to dummy's ace in order to lead the $\Diamond 3$. If East does not go up with the king, declarer can play the queen. Either West will win this trick with the ace or he will duck and be forced to win the next round. Whenever West takes his $\Diamond A$, he can do no better than to continue spades, removing declarer's last spade stopper. Eventually, when East wins with the $\Diamond K$, he won't be able to get West on lead to cash the three spade tricks.

Of course if East had won the first diamond trick with the king and played a spade, the contract would have been doomed. Declarer, by playing a low diamond off the dummy, forces East to decide whether it is better to play the king or a low diamond. In some cases a low card is correct (for example, when West holds the $\Diamond 10$ and two small diamonds). Many defenders will play low without much thought since they will be guided by the maxim 'second hand low'. If declarer had instead played a low diamond towards dummy's jack, East would have won with the king, and the contract would have been set.

In Problem 19, declarer faced a similar situation but had a simple solution: he could hold up on the first round of spades.

Good declarers consider the perspective of defenders and try to make it difficult for the defense to make the proper decisions.

**Type of play:** Sever communications.

**Inspirational features:**
1) Fear of the strong spade suit held by West.
2) Hope to have the defender with the long threatening suit win a trick and use up his entry before the suit is set up.

**Lose trick or do not try to win a trick:** —

**Create deal exercise:** Modify this exercise so that East-West have eight spades.

**North**
- ♠ J 9 8 5
- ♡ 8
- ◇ Q 10 9 8 5
- ♣ A K Q

**West**
- ♠ Q 4 3
- ♡ 10 6 5 3 2
- ◇ A 6
- ♣ 8 7 5

*Dealer E*
*Neither Vul.*

**East**
- ♠ A K 6 2
- ♡ 9 7 4
- ◇ K 4 3 2
- ♣ 6 3

**South**
- ♠ 10 7
- ♡ A K Q J
- ◇ J 7
- ♣ J 10 9 4 2

| West | North | East | South |
|------|-------|------|-------|
| | | pass | 1♣ |
| pass | 1◇ | pass | 1♡ |
| pass | 1♠ | pass | 1NT |
| pass | 3NT | all pass | |

West leads the ♡3 (phew!). You have nine winners, but the entry situation makes it difficult to enjoy them. Can you see any way to disentangle the situation?

If a partnership has a combined high card point count of 26 or more they will usually bid at least game. This general principle is very useful for beginners, but more experienced bridge players realize the many limitations of this guideline. For instance, declarer will usually make more tricks if the high card points are evenly divided between his hand and dummy's than if the points are concentrated in one hand. It is much more likely that declarer will make 3NT with 26 points if the HCP are divided 14 and 12 rather than 24 and 2. When one hand has very few HCPs and possibly no entries, there is often a problem in communication. Declarer may find himself unable to take a needed finesse or use a long suit held by the weak hand.

On the illustrated hand, North raised to 3NT with 12 HCP and a five-card suit and South became declarer with their total of 24 HCP. Unfortunately, even though the points were evenly divided on this deal, there was still a communication problem.

After seeing dummy, declarer's first reaction was a sigh of relief since the defense missed an opportunity to take the first five tricks (three spade tricks and two diamond tricks). His second reaction was to panic over the communication problem. Even though declarer appeared to have nine top tricks (five club tricks and four heart tricks), after cashing the ♣A, ♣K and ♣Q, he was stranded in dummy. There was no entry to the South hand to cash the two additional club tricks. West's opening lead of a heart had removed the one entry to the South hand. The contract went down.

Declarer could have made the contract by playing the following way. After winning the heart lead, declarer cashes his other three top heart tricks while discarding the ♣A, ♣K and ♣Q from dummy! As declarer is doing this he should take the time to observe and enjoy the shocked expressions on the faces of the three players at the table. If declarer makes these unusual discards, the success of the contract will depend on clubs breaking 3-2 (a 68% chance). Since they actually do, declarer can cash nine winning tricks and succeed in the 3NT contract.

This tactic of discarding winners to unblock a suit is called a **jettison play.** It is rare but it is worth waiting for. A jettison play is extremely easy to overlook. The correct play goes against instinct since declarers almost always discard losers rather than winners. It is very hard to throw away something valuable while keeping something that is worthless.

This problem was featured in my column in *The Bronx Journal* several years ago. Shortly after it appeared I was playing at a local club, The Bridge Deck, and missed a jettison play on a hand: even writing a column on the play could not wake me up. At the end of the hand, when I was complaining about my inability to unblock, one of the defenders, Peter Kalat, pointed out my oversight. We were both amused when I told him that I had just written a column on how easy it is to overlook a jettison play. When I think of this problem I always think of Peter. He died suddenly a few weeks prior to my sending the first draft of this book to the publisher. Peter was an extremely kind gentleman with an unbelievably warm smile. This problem on the jettison play is in his memory.

**Type of play:** Unblocking. Jettison play.

**Inspirational features:**
1) Obvious need to unblock the club suit.
2) No entries to the South hand after the first trick.

**Lose trick or do not try to win a trick:** −

**Create deal exercise:** Modify this deal so that South has a three-card heart suit.

**North**
- ♠ 6 4
- ♡ K Q J
- ◊ K Q J 8
- ♣ A 7 6 4

**West**
- ♠ K 9
- ♡ A 10 9 6 2
- ◊ A 5 2
- ♣ J 10 5

*Dealer W*
*Both Vul.*

**East**
- ♠ J 10 8
- ♡ 8 7 4
- ◊ 10 7 4 3
- ♣ 9 8 3

**South**
- ♠ A Q 7 5 3 2
- ♡ 5 3
- ◊ 9 6
- ♣ K Q 2

| West | North | East | South |
|------|-------|------|-------|
| 1♡ | 1NT | pass | 4♠ |
| all pass | | | |

West leads the ♣J. There is no way to avoid losing the two red aces, so you have to hold your trump losers to one. How will you do that?

Chess and bridge are often compared since both games require intelligence and high skill levels. However, other than that, there are more differences than similarities:
1) Chess involves playing as an individual. No communication skills are required. Bridge involves bidding and signaling during card play.
2) Chess does not involve any luck.
3) A chess tournament involves competing in several large battles. A bridge tournament involves a large number of small battles.
4) Chess is a game of complete information. Bridge players do not know the present location of all the cards.

On the illustrated deal, the success of the contract depends on holding the trump losers to one. The standard way to accomplish this, had there been no bidding by the opponents, would have been to enter dummy and take a spade finesse. This line of play will lose only one trick whenever East holds either king doubleton or king tripleton in spades. The combined chance of this occurring is 34%.

On this particular deal there is no chance that East will have either of these holdings. Since West opened the bidding, he is virtually certain to hold the ♠K, so declarer should not take the spade finesse and waste the ♠Q. Declarer must try to visualize a possible spade distribution where there is only one trump loser. The only such holding is if West started with a doubleton ♠K. Considering West's opening bid, which indicates the possession of at least five hearts, both red aces, and the ♠K, the chance of his having this spade holding is quite high. Declarer could play the ♠A followed by the ♠2 and enjoy the pleasant sight of the ♠K falling reluctantly out of West's hand on the second spade trick. Then the ♠Q will win the third round of spades and the contract will be successful.

Declarer might have had a false sense of success if the ♠K had fallen under his ace. This initial joy occurs since the ♠Q would be able to win a trick. Unfortunately, the king falling would have indicated West's singleton and therefore declarer would soon painfully realize that East started with ♠J1098 and that there are still two trump losers.

Considering the necessity of West holding king doubleton, declarer could have just as well played a small trump from his hand on the first round and when regaining the lead played the ace and queen. It would have been equally effective.

The correct line of play can only be found by counting the total HCPs in the North and South hands and visualizing the necessary enemy spade holding in order for the contract to succeed. This is an example of the type of visualization that is needed by bridge players but not by chess players.

**Type of play:** Card reading. Assumption.

**Inspirational feature:**
1) The finesse of the ♠Q is certain to lose since West opened the bidding.
2) Assume a spade holding for West where you can prevent the ♠K from capturing the queen.

**Lose trick or do not try to win a trick:** Don't try to win a trick by taking a spade finesse since it cannot succeed.

**Create deal exercise:** Modify this deal so that the defense holds the ♠A, ♠Q and ♠J and declarer should play for a singleton ace.

**North**
- ♠ Q 8 6 4 2
- ♡ 10 6 4
- ◊ A J 10
- ♣ 6 4

**West**
- ♠ J
- ♡ A K Q J
- ◊ 9 6 4 3
- ♣ Q J 10 2

*Dealer N*
*Both Vul.*

**East**
- ♠ 10 7
- ♡ 9 8 3 2
- ◊ K Q 5
- ♣ 9 8 7 3

**South**
- ♠ A K 9 5 3
- ♡ 7 5
- ◊ 8 7 2
- ♣ A K 5

| West | North | East | South |
|------|-------|------|-------|
|  | pass | pass | 1♠ |
| dbl | 4♠ | all pass |  |

West leads the ♡A, and continues the suit. You ruff the third round. How do plan to play diamonds to be certain to avoid two losers?

Often when you have a long suit you will find your partner has very few cards in that suit. You should not feel unlucky. Since there are only thirteen cards in each suit, the more you are dealt the fewer you should expect your partner to hold. On rare but happy occasions, you will have the pleasant surprise of learning that your partner has length in your suit. On the illustrated deal, when South made the bid of 1♠, North was thrilled to learn that South had been dealt at least five spades.

On the first three tricks West played top hearts, and declarer ruffed the third round. Since two heart tricks had already been lost, the success of the contract depended on holding the diamond losers to one.

The most obvious line of play is to finesse the diamond suit twice. That is, if the first finesse loses to the king or the queen, declarer returns to his hand and finesses again. This will succeed whenever the diamond king and queen are split between East and West, or when West holds both the king and the queen. The line of play will lose two tricks only when East holds both the king and the queen. If both East and West had passed throughout the bidding, the chance of success would have been approximately 75%. Since West made a takeout double, showing a good hand, West is almost certain to hold at least one of the missing diamond honors. Unfortunately, on the lie of the cards in this problem, declarer will be greatly disappointed when two diamond tricks are lost.

Declarer should choose a line which leaves no chance for the contract to fail wherever the diamond honors are located. He should play two rounds of spades, cash the ♣AK, ruff the ♣5, play a trump to return to hand and then take a diamond finesse. After East wins the ◇10 with the king or queen, East will have to choose a lead: all are awful. A diamond would play into dummy's ace-jack. A club or heart would give declarer a 'ruff and sluff'. So whatever East leads, it is impossible for declarer to lose more than one diamond trick.

A fine declarer must not only be able to execute an endplay (here, a **throw-in**), but must also be able to recognize features in a hand that suggest an endplay is possible. One feature, essential for most endplays, is a long trump suit in both declarer and dummy. This enables declarer to draw trumps, and strip his own hand and dummy of some side suits by ruffing, while still retaining at least one trump in both declarer's hand and dummy. You have to hold at least one trump in each hand in order to execute a ruff and a sluff. In addition, declarer must have a side-suit position that he wishes to have the defense lead into.

One should note that if the defense had led a diamond on any of the first three tricks the endplay would not have been possible. However, this is not an obvious play by West.

It is interesting to compare this problem with the very similar deal in Problem 6. In that problem, declarer wants the defense to take him off a club guess. On this deal, declarer knows how to play diamonds but wants to guard against the unfortunate lie of the cards when East has both the king and the queen.

**Type of play:** Endplay. Elimination (strip).

**Inspirational feature:**
1) A diamond suit that you want East to lead after the first round has been played.
2) Long trump length in both declarer and dummy.
3) The ability to strip the hand out of clubs and hearts.

**Lose trick or do not try to win a trick:** If the defense had not taken both heart tricks, declarer should play heart losers himself to try to strip the hand. Of course, if West attacks diamonds, declarer will be unable to avoid two diamond losers.

**Create deal exercise:** Modify this deal so that North has the ◇Q instead of the ◇J but the hand must still be stripped.

## PROBLEM 33  GETTING A RUFF CAN BE ROUGH

Dealer: West
Both vul.

**North**
- ♠ K 8 7
- ♡ 7 6 5
- ◊ 8 4 3
- ♣ Q J 6 2

**South**
- ♠ A Q 3
- ♡ A Q 4 3 2
- ◊ A K 6 2
- ♣ 5

| West | North | East | South |
|------|-------|------|-------|
| pass | pass | pass | 1♡ |
| pass | 2♡ | pass | 4♡ |
| all pass | | | |

West leads the ♡J. You have a trump loser, a club loser and two potential diamond losers. Can you make the hand if diamonds aren't 3-3?

## PROBLEM 34  DEFENDERS OFTEN TAKE A NAP

Dealer: East
Both vul.

**North**
- ♠ 7 4 2
- ♡ A K
- ◊ A K Q 5
- ♣ A 8 4 2

**South**
- ♠ A K 9
- ♡ Q 9 5 3
- ◊ J 6 4 2
- ♣ K Q

| West | North | East | South |
|------|-------|------|-------|
| | | pass | 1NT |
| pass | 4♣ | pass | 4♡ |
| pass | 7NT | all pass | |

West leads the ♠Q, and you survey the dummy with some regret that your bidding system hadn't been sophisticated enough to get you to 7◊ instead. How can you give yourself the best chance of thirteen tricks in notrump?

Dealer: West
Both vul.

**North**
♠ Q J
♡ A Q J 10
◇ 8 6
♣ A 7 6 3 2

**South**
♠ A K 6 4 3
♡ 6
◇ A 9 5 3 2
♣ 8 4

| West | North | East | South |
|------|-------|------|-------|
| pass | 1♣ | pass | 1♠ |
| pass | 2♣ | pass | 2◇ |
| pass | 2♡ | pass | 2NT |
| pass | 3NT | all pass | |

West leads the ♡3, and it looks as though ten tricks will be easy — five spades, three hearts and two minor-suit aces. Do you foresee any pitfalls? How will you play the hand?

Dealer: West
Both vul.

**North**
♠ K J 2
♡ 10 8 6 5 2
◇ K Q 5
♣ J 8

**South**
♠ Q 5 3
♡ K Q J 4 3
◇ A
♣ Q 10 6 4

| West | North | East | South |
|------|-------|------|-------|
| pass | pass | pass | 1♡ |
| pass | 3♡ | pass | 4♡ |
| all pass | | | |

West starts with the ♡A and continues with the ♡9. With four top losers, you have a problem. Can you see any chance of making one go away?

**North**
- ♠ K 8 7
- ♡ 7 6 5
- ◇ 8 4 3
- ♣ Q J 6 2

**West**
- ♠ 9 6 5
- ♡ J 10 9
- ◇ Q J 9 7
- ♣ K 8 7

*Dealer W*
*Both Vul.*

**East**
- ♠ J 10 4 2
- ♡ K 8
- ◇ 10 5
- ♣ A 10 9 4 3

**South**
- ♠ A Q 3
- ♡ A Q 4 3 2
- ◇ A K 6 2
- ♣ 5

| West | North | East | South |
|------|-------|------|-------|
| pass | pass | pass | 1♡ |
| pass | 2♡ | pass | 4♡ |
| all pass | | | |

West leads the ♡J. You have a trump loser, a club loser and two potential diamond losers. Can you make the hand if diamonds aren't 3-3?

In a trump contract, declarer must decide when is the best time to remove the defenders' trump cards. This timing problem is referred to as trump management. Often, plans by declarer fail due to common mistakes in timing.

On the illustrated deal, declarer is quite pleased by the trump lead. Whether or not East plays his king, declarer will be able to hold his trump losers to one trick if the heart suit splits 3-2. There is a 68% chance of this trump break occurring. Any other trump break will result in more than one trump loser.

Since declarer has a club loser and at least one heart loser, he cannot afford to lose more than one diamond trick in order for the contract to succeed. Declarer can hope that diamonds split 3-3. Such a break will result in declarer losing only one diamond, but the chance of this break is only 36%. South should not allow the success of the contract to ride on just this possibility. He should plan to ruff his fourth diamond in case the diamonds split 4-2. There is a 48% chance of such a break. Therefore, the combined chance of a 3-3 split or a 4-2 split is 84%. Pretty good.

Implementing the plan of ruffing the fourth diamond is more difficult than it seems. Here are three ways of going wrong:

1) Declarer wins the first trick with either the ace or the queen, depending on whether or not East plays the king. He then plays his other top trump. This is followed by the ◇A, the ◇K and a losing diamond on the third round of the suit. The line of play is bad technique, since when West wins the third diamond, he will play his top trump and thereby remove the last heart from dummy. Declarer will be unable to ruff the fourth diamond in dummy.

2) Declarer plays the ◇A, the ◇K, the second round of trumps, and then surrenders a diamond. This will lead to the same problem as in Case 1 and West will again pull dummy's last trump.

3) Declarer may play the ◇A and the ◇K and surrender a diamond trick before pulling the second round of trumps. We may now have something. Wrong again! When West wins the third diamond trick he will play a fourth diamond and give East a ruff.

A fine declarer will find the following successful line of play. He will give up a diamond on the second trick of the hand. Then, when declarer regains the lead, he can play a second round of trumps followed by the ◇A and the ◇K. If diamonds break 3-3, no ruff in dummy is required. If they split 4-2 and the third round of diamonds is ruffed by the defense using their master trump, dummy's last heart in dummy cannot be removed. Then declarer can eventually ruff the fourth diamond. If they break 4-2 and the third round of diamonds is not ruffed, declarer can ruff his remaining diamond in dummy. In either case with a 4-2 split, the defense will be ruffing with a natural trump trick. With proper timing this contract will always be successful whenever the trump suit splits 3-2 and diamonds split either 3-3 or 4-2.

Many possibilities had to be considered; only bridge experience and planning ahead help in these situations.

**Type of play:** Timing. Trump management.

**Inspirational feature:**
1) Very likely declarer will need a diamond ruff in dummy.
2) Fear of the defense being able to remove all dummy's trumps.
3) Fear of the defense overruffing the dummy.

**Lose trick or do not try to win a trick:** Lose a diamond trick on the second trick of hand before playing top trump cards or top diamonds.

**Create deal exercise:** Modify this deal so that the club suit can be used to avoid two diamond losers. (Hint: Look at the **Create deal exercise** for Problem 2.)

**North**
- ♠ 7 4 2
- ♡ A K
- ◇ A K Q 5
- ♣ A 8 4 2

**West**
- ♠ Q J 10 6 3
- ♡ 8 6 2
- ◇ 10 8
- ♣ 7 6 3

*Dealer E*
*Both Vul.*

**East**
- ♠ 8 5
- ♡ J 10 7 4
- ◇ 9 7 3
- ♣ J 10 9 5

**South**
- ♠ A K 9
- ♡ Q 9 5 3
- ◇ J 6 4 2
- ♣ K Q

| West | North | East | South |
|------|-------|------|-------|
| | | pass | 1NT |
| pass | 4♣ | pass | 4♡ |
| pass | 7NT | all pass | |

West leads the ♠Q, and you survey the dummy with some regret that your bidding system hadn't been sophisticated enough to get you to 7◇ instead. How can you give yourself the best chance of thirteen tricks in notrump?

Duplicate bridge players enjoy getting an excellent score on a hand in which they execute a difficult advanced play in a skillful fashion. A much less elegant way to get an excellent score occurs when declarer is given a gift by the defense. For example, suppose a declarer can win all of the remaining tricks except one. No line of play may be available to avoid losing that trick. However, if declarer simply takes his top tricks and wins the twelfth trick in his own hand (not in dummy), the defense may discard incorrectly, and that concealed last card which did not deserve to win a trick may indeed turn into a winner. This may occur because the defense had a legitimate problem. More likely, the defense took a nap during the hand. The guilty party may not be the discarder (although usually it is) since sometimes the blame can be attributed to poor signaling by his partner. The fortunate declarer will happily brag about the outcome, but will not indicate how the result was obtained.

Sometimes declarer may be able to choose a line of play that tests the defenders' alertness. Declarer may be able to make it difficult for the defense to know whether declarer's own hand or dummy's will win the twelfth trick. The illustrated deal is such an example.

Since South opened 1NT, North knew that their partnership held 35-37 points. After using Gerber to check that they had all four aces, North gambled on 7NT. Declarer has twelve top tricks: two spades, three hearts, four diamonds, and three clubs. On this deal there exists no squeeze or other skillful play that will allow declarer to make his contract. Declarer's anguish is increased by the realization that a 7◊ contract would almost always succeed if diamonds split 3-2.

Suppose declarer takes the following eight tricks: ♠K, ♣K and ♣Q, ♡A and ♡K, ♣A (discard spade), ♠A, and ♡Q (discard spade). This will leave South with four diamonds and the ♡9 and North with four diamonds and the ♣8. East will hold three diamonds, the ♣J, and the ♡J. If declarer now cashes the ◊A, ◊K and ◊Q, there is a big difference between playing the ◊2, ◊4 and ◊J from South or following with the ◊2, ◊6 and ◊J. Whether South retains the ◊4 or the ◊6 will control where the twelfth trick will be won. East will be faced with an uncomfortable problem when the ◊5 is played from dummy on the twelfth trick. A decent defender will know that South has a heart loser and will see the club loser in dummy. But where, oh where, will the twelfth trick be won? Unless East foresaw this problem developing, and closely watched which diamonds were played by West and South, he will have a sinking feeling in his stomach and will say a silent prayer as he guesses which jack to discard.

Declarer could have made this problem for East even harder by playing two rounds of diamonds earlier in the play. At that time, East would have been less likely to appreciate the importance of observing the diamond spot cards. This deal may look familiar to some readers: I used the same example in *A Bridge to Simple Squeezes*. I don't like to waste good material!

**Type of play:** Memory squeeze.

**Inspirational feature:**
1) Threat cards in hearts and clubs.
2) Lack of necessary communication for a legitimate squeeze.
3) Even though no legitimate squeeze is available, declarer can make a defender's life difficult.

**Lose trick or do not try to win a trick:** −

**Create deal exercise:** Modify this deal so that East is a victim of a legitimate simple squeeze in clubs and hearts.

**North**
- ♠ Q J
- ♡ A Q J 10
- ◊ 8 6
- ♣ A 7 6 3 2

**West**
- ♠ 7 5
- ♡ 9 8 5 3 2
- ◊ 7 4
- ♣ K J 10 5

Dealer W
Both Vul.

**East**
- ♠ 10 9 8 2
- ♡ K 7 4
- ◊ K Q J 10
- ♣ Q 9

**South**
- ♠ A K 6 4 3
- ♡ 6
- ◊ A 9 5 3 2
- ♣ 8 4

| West | North | East | South |
|------|-------|------|-------|
| pass | 1♣ | pass | 1♠ |
| pass | 2♣ | pass | 2◊ |
| pass | 2♡ | pass | 2NT |
| pass | 3NT | all pass | |

West leads the ♡3, and it looks as though ten tricks will be easy — five spades, three hearts and two minor-suit aces. Do you foresee any pitfalls? How will you play the hand?

A misfit is a situation that occurs when one player has two long suits and two short suits, and his partner also has two long suits and two short suits, but the long suits in each hand correspond to the short suits in his partner's hand. In effect, this is a situation where there is no fit.

When a misfit occurs a partnership might possess the high card values for game but no game contract can be made. Since that pair will lack an appropriate trump suit they will often have no recourse but to attempt a notrump contract. Unfortunately, a notrump contract is far from a safe haven on misfit hands. A potential major problem is lack of communication between declarer and dummy.

The bidding sequence revealed the values for game, but the hand was clearly a misfit. During the bidding, the search for a reasonable trump fit forced both North and South to face several awkward bidding situations.

When declarer saw dummy and the opening lead, he was extremely pleased with the contract. In spite of the misfit, with proper technique this hand plays nicely in notrump. Declarer expected to win ten tricks provided that spades did not break worse than 4-2: one club, one diamond, three hearts and five spades. He quickly called for the ♡10 based more on instinct than analysis. East won that trick, and played the ◇K. This was a fatal blow to declarer. The ◇A was a crucial entry to declarer's hand. Declarer had hoped to be able to cash the ♠Q and the ♠J in dummy and then use the ◇A as an entry to his hand in order to cash at least two but more likely three additional spade tricks. Instead, he won the ◇K with the ace and had no recourse but to pray for a 3-3 spade break (36% chance). He cashed the ♠Q and overtook the jack with the ace in order to enter his hand and attempt to run the spades. When spades broke 4-2, declarer was doomed to defeat since he could only win eight tricks.

Declarer could not have avoided the communication problem by ducking the ◇K, since the defense would have continued diamonds for a second round. If declarer were to duck that second round of diamonds, the defense would shift to a different suit, since a third round of diamonds by the defense would enable declarer to develop a second diamond trick.

As so often is the case, declarer's mistake took place on the first trick. He should have won the opening lead with the ♡A, cashed the ♠Q and the ♠J, and then played the hearts until the defense took the king. With this line of play, declarer would not have been vulnerable to the communication problem.

The finesse was pointless. Even if it had been successful, it could not have been repeated. So, unless the lead was from king-doubleton, a heart trick would still have to be surrendered. Besides, West would never lead low from king doubleton.

A recurring theme in these problems is to plan a whole hand, before calling for a card from dummy on the first trick. Even experienced players get sloppy. Always consider potential communication problems, particularly when you face a misfit.

**Type of play:** Entry management.

**Inspirational feature:**
1) Misfits create entry problems.
2) Fear of the defense forcing declarer to play the ◇A prematurely.

**Lose trick or do not try to win a trick:** Since declarer must cash the ♠Q and the ♠J prior to losing the heart trick, he must not try to win with a pointless finesse.

**Create deal exercise:** Modify the deal so that North has the heart king.

**North**
- ♠ K J 2
- ♡ 10 8 6 5 2
- ◇ K Q 5
- ♣ J 8

**West**
- ♠ A 9 7
- ♡ A 9
- ◇ J 8 7 4
- ♣ 9 7 3 2

*Dealer W*
*Both Vul.*

**East**
- ♠ 10 8 6 4
- ♡ 7
- ◇ 10 9 6 3 2
- ♣ A K 5

**South**
- ♠ Q 5 3
- ♡ K Q J 4 3
- ◇ A
- ♣ Q 10 6 4

| West | North | East | South |
|------|-------|------|-------|
| pass | pass | pass | 1♡ |
| pass | 3♡ | pass | 4♡ |
| all pass | | | |

West starts with the ♡A and continues with the ♡9. With four top losers, you have a problem. Can you see any chance of making one go away?

When two bridge players form a new partnership, it is essential for them to establish their understanding of responder's double raise after partner has opened the bidding. There are three common understandings associated with a double raise in a major. In the 1950s when the Goren System was very popular, a 3♡ bid after a 1♡ bid showed good heart support with 13 to 15 points. It was, of course, game forcing. This understanding is still used by many rubber bridge players but by very few duplicate players. In the 1970s many duplicate partnerships started using the double raise to show invitational hands with trump support and 10 to 12 points. A third alternative, which has gained popularity over the past fifteen years, is to employ the double raise with at least four-card trump support but at most 7 points. The purpose of this weak double raise is to interfere with the opponents' ability to find their best fit.

On the illustrated hand, by partnership agreement, North revealed an invitational hand with three or more hearts with the double raise to 3♡. South confidently bid 4♡.

South was not pleased when dummy hit the table. Declarer was disappointed to find North with 5 points in diamonds where they were not helpful. There are four fast losers: one spade, one heart, and two clubs. Declarer can discard two cards on the top diamonds in dummy, but unfortunately, he is still stuck with the same four losers. The discards are useless. Or are they?

After West won the first trick, he continued with the ♡9. Declarer won the trick in the South hand and led the ♠3. Declarer was hoping that West held the ♠A and would duck this spade trick. West suddenly was faced with a difficult decision. He decided not to play the ace and played the ♠7 – a very reasonable choice looking at dummy. For example, South might have held just two low spades and made the incorrect guess of playing the jack from dummy. On the illustrated deal, the spade duck was what declarer had been hoping would happen. Declarer's prayers were answered. After winning that spade trick with the jack, declarer cashed the ♢A, returned to dummy with a trump, and discarded two spades on dummy's winning diamonds. Declarer then conceded two club tricks and crossruffed the last four tricks. The 4♡ contract was successful.

It turned out that the two diamond discards were useful after all. It was essential first to sneak a trick past the defender with the ♠A before taking the two discards. If South had discarded two spades on the diamonds before playing a spade trick, the defense would not have let the spade trick get past them. Give the defense their tough decisions before revealing your hand.

**Type of play:** Deception.

**Inspirational feature:**
1) Discarding two spades on the two top diamonds does not avoid the spade loser unless a round of spades is ducked by the defense.
2) Appreciating the difficult problem that can be created for West when the ♠3 is led.

**Lose trick or do not try to win a trick:** –

**Create deal exercise:** Modify this deal so that East opens the bidding 1♢ and spades should be played differently.

Dealer: East
Both vul.

**North**
- ♠ K 6
- ♡ A J 10 8
- ◊ A K 3
- ♣ K J 5 2

**South**
- ♠ A 3 2
- ♡ K Q 9 6 4 3
- ◊ 7.5 2
- ♣ 10

| West | North | East | South |
|------|-------|------|-------|
|      |       | 1◊   | 1♡    |
| pass | 4NT   | pass | 5♠    |
| pass | 6♡    | all pass |    |

West leads the ◊9. You will be able to ruff a spade in dummy, but where is that diamond loser going to go?

Dealer: West
Neither vul.

**North**
♠ 9 2
♡ 8 7 4
◇ 7 5 3
♣ A K J 5 3

**South**
♠ A K Q J 5 4 3
♡ A 9 3
◇ A K Q
♣ —

| West | North | East | South |
|------|-------|------|-------|
| pass | pass | pass | 2♣ |
| pass | 3♣ | pass | 6♠ |
| all pass | | | |

West leads the ◇10. If only you could use dummy's club honors somehow…
How will you play this hand?

**North**
- ♠ K 6
- ♡ A J 10 8
- ◇ A K 3
- ♣ K J 5 2

**West**
- ♠ 10 9 7 5 4
- ♡ 5 2
- ◇ 9 6
- ♣ 7 6 4 3

*Dealer E*
*Both Vul.*

**East**
- ♠ Q J 8
- ♡ 7
- ◇ Q J 10 8 4
- ♣ A Q 9 8

**South**
- ♠ A 3 2
- ♡ K Q 9 6 4 3
- ◇ 7 5 2
- ♣ 10

| West | North | East | South |
|------|-------|------|-------|
| | | 1◇ | 1♡ |
| pass | 4NT | pass | 5♠ |
| pass | 6♡ | all pass | |

West leads the ◇9. You will be able to ruff a spade in dummy, but where is that diamond loser going to go?

One of the first conventions new bridge players learn is Blackwood. Most tournament players use some variant of Blackwood. A popular alternative is called **Roman Keycard Blackwood,** where the king of the trump suit is treated with the same respect as the four aces. A 4NT bid asks partner about his possession of these five keycards. When using this variation of Blackwood the typical responses are as follows:

5♣: 0 or 3 keycards
5◇: 1 or 4 keycards
5♡: 2 or 5 keycards without the queen of trumps
5♠: 2 or 5 keycards with the queen of trumps

Some partnerships use 5♣ to show 1 or 4, and 5◇ to show 0 or 3.

On the illustrated hand, North was very optimistic when he decided to investigate slam possibilities. He was extremely fortunate to learn that South had the trump queen and two of the three missing keycards. With this information he bid 6♡. Actually, after the 5♠ response, he had no choice. With this form of Blackwood, North has to be prepared to go to the six-level if his partner holds two keycards and the trump queen. Of course, North does not know whether South has two aces or one ace and the ♠K.

There are two potential losers: a diamond and a club. Since declarer and dummy have a total of 28 HCPs and East made an opening bid, declarer realizes that both the ace and queen of clubs are held by East, behind the king and jack. Armed with this knowledge and the powerful ♣10, he realizes he holds a potential club trick. After winning the diamond lead, declarer plays two rounds of hearts ending in his hand. He then leads the ♣10 and plays the ♣2 from dummy. Of course, as expected, this trick is lost to the queen. After winning the diamond return in dummy, declarer leads the ♣K. When East does not play the ♣A, declarer confidently discards a diamond from the South hand. If East had played the ♣A, declarer would have ruffed and eventually entered dummy to throw his diamond loser on the ♣J.

The play of the ♣K with the intent of discarding a diamond if the ace does not appear is called a **ruffing finesse**. The information that declarer learned from East's 1◊ bid made it a sure thing. Even if East had not opened the bidding, and declarer had no information about which defender held the club honors, the same technique should be used in the club suit. This method has approximately a 75% chance of success. It will only fail if East holds the ♣Q and West holds the ♣A (and ducks the first round of the suit).

A ruffing finesse usually involves two touching honors (such as king-queen) opposite a void.

On this hand, however, it was necessary to drive out the ♣Q with the ♣10 in order to create a card combination where a ruffing finesse was available. I hope you have enough bridge finesse to recognize a ruffing finesse.

**Type of play:** Ruffing finesse. Card reading.

**Inspirational feature:**
1) Knowledge of the location of the ♣A.
2) Recognizing that losing a club to the queen will set up a ruffing finesse that is virtually guaranteed to be successful.
3) The slow diamond loser. After the diamond lead, it is essential that this loser is a third-round loser rather than a second.

**Lose trick or do not try to win a trick:** By losing a club trick, declarer can set up the card combination for a ruffing finesse.

**Create deal exercise:** Modify this deal so that declarer has two slow diamond losers where one of them can be avoided by a ruffing finesse in clubs.

**North**
- ♠ 9 2
- ♡ 8 7 4
- ◇ 7 5 3
- ♣ A K J 5 3

**West**
- ♠ 10 7
- ♡ 10 6 5 2
- ◇ 10 9 8 6
- ♣ Q 10 7

**East**
- ♠ 8 6
- ♡ K Q J
- ◇ J 4 2
- ♣ 9 8 6 4 2

Dealer W
Neither Vul.

**South**
- ♠ A K Q J 5 4 3
- ♡ A 9 3
- ◇ A K Q
- ♣ —

| West | North | East | South |
|------|-------|------|-------|
| pass | pass | pass | 2♣ |
| pass | 3♣ | pass | 6♠ |
| all pass | | | |

West leads the ◇10. If only you could use dummy's club honors somehow... How will you play this hand?

It is a pleasure to feel the adrenalin rush of a great hand. Such a hand is all too rare. The chance of being dealt 23+ HCP is 0.214%. This means you are lucky if you pick up one 23+ HCP hand in every 400 deals. Actually with eleven probable winners in just the South hand it is a great 23-point hand. Does this imply that there exist bad 23-point hands? Maybe, but don't expect any sympathy when you hold one.

Most players use a 2♣ opening bid as an artificial bid showing a very powerful hand. It does not give any information about the hand except its strength. This system frees the rest of the two-level to be used for weak two-bids. Powerful hands are often hard to bid, so one should take comfort that at least the first bid is easy: simply 2♣.

The illustrated hand is clearly appropriate for a 2♣ bid. The 3♣ response shows a club suit and at least 8 HCP. Since North had previously passed, his strength is limited. South feared that North's club strength might have limited usefulness opposite his club void. He therefore chose not to consider a seven-level contract, but was content to jump to 6♠.

When dummy hit the table it became clear that South's fears were justified. Dummy is a real tease. Declarer can reach out and touch those beautiful clubs, but has a problem getting to dummy to use them.

After winning the diamond lead, declarer should lead a small spade toward the ♠9 in dummy. If West holds the ♠10, he will probably win the trick. After declarer wins the next trick, he can lead another small spade to dummy's ♠9. This will enable South to discard his two heart losers on North's club winners. If West does not grab that trick with the ♠10, declarer will play the ♠9 and win all thirteen tricks. You probably are thinking that of course West will play the ♠10. Why would he not? Well, by ducking, West may trick declarer into concluding that East has the ♠10; the only hope, therefore, is to play the ♠2 and pray that East has a singleton ♠10. A more likely reason that West might not play the ♠10 is his state of complete surprise. West may play the ♠7 before he realizes that the ♠10 can actually win the trick. Try explaining that duck to partner.

South will probably feel a tinge of pain losing a trump trick while holding such a trump powerhouse. It is, however, the necessary play to develop an entry to dummy. Declarer's pain would be much greater if East were the defender holding the ♠10; in that case, declarer would go down two tricks. He would have to console himself with the thought that he had no choice but to gamble and try to make this slam.

If the opening lead by the defense had been a heart, declarer would have faced much poorer prospects. With that lead, declarer must play a top trump and hope that one of the defenders has the singleton ♠10. With such good fortune the ♠9 would be an entry to dummy. The probability of a singleton ♠10 is only 12%.

Don't have a blind spot when looking at the spots on a spot card. They often can be developed into winners. This is particularly useful when searching for entries.

**Type of play:** Entry management.

**Inspirational feature:**
1) The ♠9 is the closest card declarer has to an entry in dummy.
2) Not being willing to accept wasting the ♣A and the ♣K.
3) Two slow losers in hearts. (Without that the trump play is really silly!)

**Lose trick or do not try to win a trick:** The mother of all hands where declarer should lose a trick that could have been won.

**Create deal exercise:** Modify this deal so that declarer is certain of an entry to dummy in the trump suit even though dummy does not hold a trump winner.

Throughout this book I have used my heavy-handed, repetitive style to hammer home several important issues in declarer play. Even that sentence was repetitive.

This book demonstrates many situations where the key play requires losing a trick. What could violate bridge instinct more than losing a trump trick, as in Problem 38, in order to obtain an entry?

When planning the play of a hand, slow losers may aid declarer in finding the correct line of play. This book heavily emphasizes declarer's ability to avoid them. Sometimes the issue is not only that declarer possesses a slow loser but also on which round of the suit the loser will occur.

Consider the following example where declarer is in 6♠ and the opening lead is the ♣K. What should declarer discard from his hand on that first trick?

Dummy
♠ K J 10 5
♡ J 3 2
◇ J 3 2
♣ A 5 4

Declarer
♠ A Q 9 8 7 4 2
♡ A Q 4
◇ A Q 4
♣ —

The answer is nothing. Sorry, this was a trick question. I feel guilty, but I hope it will make my point easier to remember. On the first trick, declarer should play a small club from dummy and ruff in his own hand. At some future time, when declarer will have learned what to discard, he will take the discard on the ♣A.

After ruffing the club lead and entering dummy with a trump winner, declarer can play a small diamond to the queen. Even if the finesse is successful, unless East started with king doubleton or singleton, declarer will still have one diamond loser since East can cover the jack with the king. The chance that East started with doubleton or singleton king is approximately 5%.

With this diamond holding a successful finesse does not avoid a loser, but a successful finesse will result in shifting the loser to the third round. A third-round loser will mean that the one discard available with the ♣A will enable declarer to avoid losing any tricks in the diamond suit.

Obviously, since both red suits are identical, declarer could have played the heart suit instead of the diamond suit. Whichever suit declarer starts with will inform him on how to discard on the ♣A. If the finesse of the queen fails, discard a card in the other red suit. Of course that discard will only prove useful if the finesse in the other red suit is successful.

Suppose dummy started with both the ♣A and the ♣K. Now, if the first finesse fails, declarer should discard two cards from the other red side suit and avoid the second finesse. If the finesse succeeds and the king does not fall under the ace on the second round, discard one card from each red suit. This will enable declarer to make all thirteen tricks if the finesse in the other red suit is also successful.

In this example, playing the ♣A should be postponed until declarer knows the best way to take advantage of it. A common situation that requires this play occurs when declarer has some fear that a defender will ruff a winner in dummy. Then it is best not to play the winner but instead to ruff, pull all of the defenders' trump cards, and then play dummy's winner for a discard.

Sometimes declarer is unable to recognize whether a card is a winner or a loser. In that case declarer must delay taking a discard. Consider the following example where declarer is in 7♠ and the opening lead is the ♣K.

Dummy
♠ K J 10
♡ K 3 2
♢ K 3 2
♣ A 5 4 2

Declarer
♠ A Q 9 8 7
♡ A Q 5 4
♢ A Q 5 4
♣ —

On this first trick, declarer will not know whether either of the red suits is splitting 3-3. After learning that a suit is breaking 3-3, declarer will know to discard the spot card in the other red suit. If that suit were to also break 3-3, declarer will have fourteen top tricks and will wish to carry one over to the next hand.

If neither red suit splits 3-3, declarer may have the opportunity to execute a squeeze. I'm not going to go into a full description of the potential squeeze since I want to sell you my book, *A Bridge to Simple Squeezes*. Actually, the real reason is that it is not the point I am trying to make here. If you would like to find the squeeze, here are some hints. The two threat cards are the fourth cards in both red suits. The squeeze card is the ♣A. It is a positional squeeze against East. Obviously, the ♣A cannot be played on the first round.

This hand has all the inspirational features that appeared in Problem 23 for a dummy reversal. That line of play, where the three small clubs in dummy get ruffed by declarer's spades, will yield thirteen tricks whenever the trump suit splits 3-2. There is a 68% chance of that split. The alternative line of play, where declarer will succeed if either red suit splits 3-3 or East can be squeezed, has about the same chance of success. Tough decision, but bridge is a tough game.

Very often I make my first bridge mistake before I even get to the first deal. The local club where I do most of my playing is *The Bridge Deck* in Scarsdale. I have driven to this bridge club several hundred times. Often I pick up one of my partners who lives ten minutes from the club. I have picked up this partner dozens of times. Whether or not I am picking him up, the first half of my drive is identical but then I face a decision where I must choose one highway to pick him up or the other one to go directly to the club. Obviously, I don't need my car navigation system to get me to either destination. Very often I find myself heading for the club while my partner is still standing in front of his home. I quickly realize my error, curse at myself, pound my head with my palm, and go back to pick him up.

Why do I make this error so often? I am not old enough to blame it on my age.

My problem is that I let habit control me. I am driving on automatic pilot. I know that I am heading for a session of bridge and nothing is inspiring me to ask the important question, 'Do I need to pick up my partner?' I don't forget, but I just don't think about it at the right time.

Experienced players develop a stockpile of standard routine actions. One can achieve a reasonably high level of performance by just calling on that reservoir of information. New players lack that stockpile. Often, if I am playing against beginners in the last round of an event, I will ask them if they are enjoying themselves. Usually I get a positive response but invariably it includes, 'I'm glad this is the last round. I am exhausted.' Why are they so tired? At their level they have to concentrate on every bid and play, no matter how obvious. They lack the stockpile of responses that experienced players often rely on.

Even though experienced players have developed a warehouse of automatic actions, they must not let themselves be guided totally by habit. The main goal of *A Bridge to Inspired Declarer Play* is to help the reader identify features that should inspire a declarer to the correct line of play and help him resist relying too heavily on habit and instinct. The ability to execute a play is useless unless one can appreciate that the play is appropriate for a particular hand.

# SECTION 2
## Sample Answers to "Create Alternative Deal" Exercises

## PROBLEM 1

**North**
- ♠ Q 4 3 2
- ♡ J 10 5
- ◇ J 8 7
- ♣ K 5 3

**West**
- ♠ J 10 9 8
- ♡ 8 2
- ◇ A K Q
- ♣ Q J 8 6

*Dealer N*
*EW Vul.*

**East**
- ♠ A K 7
- ♡ 7 6 3
- ◇ 9 6 5 2
- ♣ 10 9 7

**South**
- ♠ 6 5
- ♡ A K Q 9 4
- ◇ 10 4 3
- ♣ A 4 2

| West | North | East | South |
|------|-------|------|-------|
|      | pass  | pass | 1♡    |
| dbl  | 2♡    | all pass |   |

Opening lead: ◇A (The defense cashes three diamonds and shifts to the ♠J.)

Don't play the ♠Q until it is a winner on the fourth round. The ◇K was shifted in order to give West the values for a double. Of course, a club shift at Trick 4 would defeat the contract.

## PROBLEM 2

**North**
- ♠ Q 10 9 2
- ♡ 9 7
- ◇ K 6 5 4
- ♣ Q J 3

**West**
- ♠ 6 3
- ♡ J 6 4 3
- ◇ Q J 9 7
- ♣ A K 9

*Dealer W*
*EW Vul.*

**East**
- ♠ 5
- ♡ A 10 8 5 2
- ◇ 10
- ♣ 10 8 7 6 4 2

**South**
- ♠ A K J 8 7 4
- ♡ K Q
- ◇ A 8 3 2
- ♣ 5

| West | North | East | South |
|------|-------|------|-------|
| pass | pass  | pass | 1♠    |
| pass | 2♠    | pass | 4♠    |
| all pass |   |   |   |

Opening lead: ♣A, followed by the ◇Q

Declarer must discard a diamond from South on both club honors. If the diamonds had split 3-2 this play would not have gained anything, but when they are 4-1 the loser on loser play is necessary in order to avoid two diamond losers.

## PROBLEM 3

**North**
- ♠ Q J 4
- ♡ 6 5 3
- ◇ K Q J 10 3
- ♣ 7 4

**West**
- ♠ 10 9 6 3
- ♡ Q J 7
- ◇ 8 2
- ♣ Q 8 3 2

*Dealer W*
*Neither Vul.*

**East**
- ♠ K 7 5
- ♡ 10 9 8 2
- ◇ A 6 5
- ♣ J 10 9

**South**
- ♠ A 8 2
- ♡ A K 4
- ◇ 9 7 4
- ♣ A K 6 5

| West | North | East | South |
|------|-------|------|-------|
| pass | pass | pass | 1♣ |
| pass | 1◇ | pass | 2NT |
| pass | 3NT | all pass | |

Opening lead: ♠3

Declarer must be careful to win the first trick with the ♠A even if the first trick can be won with the ♠8. If South does not play the ace on the first trick, he will lose his spade entry to dummy.

## PROBLEM 4

**North**
- ♠ K 8
- ♡ A K 3
- ◇ 6 5 4 3 2
- ♣ A 7 4

**West**
- ♠ 9 4
- ♡ Q 10 8
- ◇ K J 10 9
- ♣ Q J 10 6

*Dealer E*
*Both Vul.*

**East**
- ♠ 2
- ♡ J 9 5 4 2
- ◇ A Q 8 7
- ♣ 9 8 3

**South**
- ♠ A Q J 10 7 6 5 3
- ♡ 7 6
- ◇ —
- ♣ K 5 2

| West | North | East | South |
|------|-------|------|-------|
| | | pass | 4♠ |
| pass | 5♣ | pass | 5◇ |
| pass | 7♠ | all pass | |

Opening lead: ♣Q

With your outstanding trump holding, you will feel a little embarrassed if your ♠8 loses to the ♠9, but that weird looking finesse is necessary for that essential fifth entry to dummy. North was very aggressive in bidding the grand.

## PROBLEM 5

**North**
- ♠ 8 6 5
- ♡ K J 4 3 2
- ◇ Q 8 7
- ♣ J 7

**West**
- ♠ 7 3
- ♡ A 9 5
- ◇ 9 6
- ♣ A 9 8 5 4 3

*Dealer N*
*EW Vul.*

**East**
- ♠ A K J 10 4 2
- ♡ Q 10 8
- ◇ 4 3
- ♣ 6 2

**South**
- ♠ Q 9
- ♡ 7 6
- ◇ A K J 10 5 2
- ♣ K Q 10

| West | North | East | South |
|------|-------|------|-------|
|      | pass  | 2♠   | 3◇    |
| all pass |   |      |       |

Opening lead: ♠7

After East cashes the two top spades, declarer should infer that West has the ace of hearts, without needing the discovery play. East opened 2♠ rather than 1♠ with 8 points in spades so declarer should assume East does not have another ace.

## PROBLEM 6

**North**
- ♠ Q 10 9 2
- ♡ J 7 5
- ◇ 9 7 6
- ♣ K 10 3

**West**
- ♠ 5 4
- ♡ Q 10 9 8 6
- ◇ K Q J 3
- ♣ 8 5

*Dealer W*
*Neither Vul.*

**East**
- ♠ 6
- ♡ A K
- ◇ 10 8 5 4 2
- ♣ J 9 7 6 4

**South**
- ♠ A K J 8 7 3
- ♡ 4 3 2
- ◇ A
- ♣ A Q 2

| West | North | East | South |
|------|-------|------|-------|
| pass | pass  | pass | 1♠    |
| pass | 2♠    | pass | 4♠    |
| all pass |   |      |       |

Opening lead: ◇K

Declarer can strip the hand by drawing trumps, ruffing diamonds and cashing the club winners. Now when declarer plays a heart, after East cashes the ace and king he will be endplayed and have to surrender a ruff and a sluff

**North**
- ♠ A 4 2
- ♡ J 3
- ◇ 7 6 5
- ♣ 10 9 7 6 5

| West | North | East | South |
|------|-------|------|-------|
|      |       | 2♠   | 3♡    |
| all pass |   |      |       |

**West**
- ♠ 8
- ♡ 7 6 4
- ◇ K Q J 4 2
- ♣ K Q J 2

Dealer E
Neither Vul.

**East**
- ♠ Q J 10 9 7 6
- ♡ A 8
- ◇ 10 9 8
- ♣ 8 3

Opening lead: ♠8

With this bidding, declarer must win the first trick with the king. When East wins the trump ace, he can only give West a ruff of a loser.

**South**
- ♠ K 5 3
- ♡ K Q 10 9 5 2
- ◇ A 3
- ♣ A 4

**North**
- ♠ 9 6 3 2
- ♡ A 9
- ◇ A 10 4 2
- ♣ A 5 3

| West | North | East | South |
|------|-------|------|-------|
| 3♠   | pass  | pass | 4♡    |
| pass | 6♡    | all pass |   |

**West**
- ♠ A K J 10 8 7 5
- ♡ 6
- ◇ J 9 7 6 5
- ♣ —

Dealer W
EW Vul.

**East**
- ♠ 4
- ♡ 7 5 3 2
- ◇ 8
- ♣ Q J 10 9 8 7 6

Opening lead: ♠A

When West shows out on the first round of clubs, declarer will know that West has five diamonds. Declarer doesn't really need the count since East will show out on the second round of diamonds and South will know to finesse (a marked finesse).

**South**
- ♠ Q
- ♡ K Q J 10 8 4
- ◇ K Q 3
- ♣ K 4 2

**North**
♠ 6 2
♡ 4 3 2
◇ 8 4 2
♣ 9 8 5 4 3

**West**
♠ K Q J 9 8 7 4
♡ 9
◇ 9 7
♣ K 10 2

*Dealer W*
*Both Vul.*

**East**
♠ 10
♡ 8 6 5
◇ Q J 10 5 3
♣ A Q J 6

**South**
♠ A 5 3
♡ A K Q J 10 7
◇ A K 6
♣ 7

| West | North | East | South |
|------|-------|------|-------|
| 3♠ | pass | pass | 4♡ |
| all pass | | | |

Opening lead: ♠K

Declarer must assume that East started with five diamonds or East would be able to discard two diamonds on spade tricks, and overruff the third round of diamonds.

**North**
♠ A 5 3 2
♡ A 5 4 2
◇ A J 8
♣ A K

**West**
♠ J 10 9 8 6
♡ J 10 9 8
◇ 7 2
♣ 8 4

*Dealer E*
*Both Vul.*

**East**
♠ 7
♡ 7 6
◇ 10 9 6 5
♣ Q J 10 9 7 3

**South**
♠ K Q 4
♡ K Q 3
◇ K Q 4 3
♣ 6 5 2

| West | North | East | South |
|------|-------|------|-------|
| | | pass | 1NT |
| pass | 7NT | all pass | |

Opening lead: ♠J

On the fourth diamond trick, West will be squeezed. It is, however, necessary for declarer to play either three top hearts or three top spades before playing the fourth diamond. Are you confused? I'm sorry, but my squeeze book explains this potential mistake.[1]

1. The original squeeze in this problem will work against either defender and is called an **automatic squeeze**. The squeeze in the layout above, with the spade and heart threat cards both in the North hand, will only work against West and is called a **positional squeeze**.

## PROBLEM 11

**North**
- ♠ J 10 6 4 2
- ♡ A 9 5
- ◇ K 4 3
- ♣ A 5

**West**
- ♠ A 7
- ♡ J 10 2
- ◇ A J 7 6
- ♣ K Q J 8

*Dealer E*
*NS Vul.*

**East**
- ♠ 5
- ♡ 7 6 4 3
- ◇ 9 5 2
- ♣ 7 6 4 3 2

**South**
- ♠ K Q 9 8 3
- ♡ K Q 8
- ◇ Q 10 8
- ♣ 10 9

| West | North | East | South |
|------|-------|------|-------|
|      |       | pass | 1♠ |
| 1NT[1] | 4♠ | all pass | |

1. 16-18 HCP.

Opening lead: ♣K

Play diamonds by leading the ◇10 from the South hand. Let it ride if West does not cover with the jack. If West covers, win the king and play a low diamond toward the Q-8.

Note: This contract can also be made on an endplay. Win first trick. Strip the defenders of their hearts and spades. If West did not take the club winner after winning the ♠A, put West in with the club loser. If West took the club winner, after stripping the hand, lead the ◇Q to endplay West. All the inspirational features for endplays that appeared in Problem 6 are present.

## PROBLEM 12

**North**
- ♠ A 10 8
- ♡ Q 10 8 5 2
- ◇ 7
- ♣ 7 5 4 2

**West**
- ♠ Q J 7
- ♡ 7
- ◇ A 10 4 3 2
- ♣ K 10 9 8

*Dealer S*
*EW Vul.*

**East**
- ♠ 9 6 5 4 2
- ♡ A
- ◇ J 9 8 6
- ♣ A Q J

**South**
- ♠ K 3
- ♡ K J 9 6 4 3
- ◇ K Q 5
- ♣ 6 3

| West | North | East | South |
|------|-------|------|-------|
|      |       |      | 1♡ |
| pass | 4♡ | all pass | |

Opening lead: ♠Q

The ♠K is the only immediate entry to hand. South must take a spade finesse on the second trick and discard a club on the ♠A. If South plays trump before the spade finesse, the defense can win that trick and gobble up a fast diamond loser and two fast club losers.

## PROBLEM 13

**North**
- ♠ K Q J
- ♡ 8 4 3
- ♢ A K 7 5 3
- ♣ K 5

**West**
- ♠ 6 5
- ♡ K J 9
- ♢ Q 9 8
- ♣ Q 10 6 3 2

*Dealer E*
*EW Vul.*

**East**
- ♠ 9 2
- ♡ A Q 10 2
- ♢ J 10
- ♣ J 9 8 7 4

**South**
- ♠ A 10 8 7 4 3
- ♡ 7 6 5
- ♢ 6 4 2
- ♣ A

| West | North | East | South |
|------|-------|------|-------|
|  |  | pass | 2♠ |
| pass | 2NT | pass | 3♠[1] |
| pass | 4♠ | all pass |  |

1. Playing the version of Ogust described in the Problem.

Opening lead: ♠6

Throw a diamond on the ♣K. Now if diamonds split 3-2, two hearts can be discarded.

## PROBLEM 14

**North**
- ♠ 9 6 5
- ♡ K 7 6 4 3
- ♢ 6
- ♣ A 8 4 2

**West**
- ♠ K 8 7 3
- ♡ —
- ♢ K 10 9 5
- ♣ K 7 6 5 3

*Dealer W*
*EW Vul.*

**East**
- ♠ A Q 10
- ♡ Q J 10
- ♢ Q J 8 3
- ♣ Q 10 9

**South**
- ♠ J 4 2
- ♡ A 9 8 5 2
- ♢ A 7 4 2
- ♣ J

| West | North | East | South |
|------|-------|------|-------|
| pass | pass | 1♢ | 1♡ |
| dbl | 4♡ | all pass |  |

Opening lead: ♢5

Declarer plays two rounds of hearts. Since East has the remaining heart, declarer fears East will overruff a diamond and cash three spades. If declarer starts with a club ruff, East can discard a diamond on the fourth round of clubs and then overruff a diamond. If declarer starts with a diamond ruff this cannot happen.

## PROBLEM 15

**North**
- ♠ J 5 3
- ♡ J 10 5
- ◇ K 5 3 2
- ♣ K 6 4

**West**
- ♠ A K Q 10
- ♡ 4 3
- ◇ J 10 8
- ♣ 10 8 5 3

*Dealer W*
*Both Vul.*

**East**
- ♠ 9 8 4
- ♡ 9 8 7 6 2
- ◇ A 9
- ♣ Q J 9

**South**
- ♠ 7 6 2
- ♡ A K Q
- ◇ Q 7 6 4
- ♣ A 7 2

| West | North | East | South |
|------|-------|------|-------|
| pass | pass | pass | 1NT |
| pass | 2NT | all pass | |

Opening lead: ♠A

You can only take three diamond tricks but you will still win eight tricks.

## PROBLEM 16

**North**
- ♠ A 8 4
- ♡ Q 5
- ◇ J 9 5 4
- ♣ J 7 4 2

**West**
- ♠ K Q J 10 6
- ♡ K 8
- ◇ 10 6 3 2
- ♣ 9 3

*Dealer N*
*Both Vul.*

**East**
- ♠ 9
- ♡ J 10 9 7 6 3
- ◇ 8 7
- ♣ 10 8 6 5

**South**
- ♠ 7 5 3 2
- ♡ A 4 2
- ◇ A K Q
- ♣ A K Q

| West | North | East | South |
|------|-------|------|-------|
| | pass | pass | 2♣ |
| pass | 2◇ | pass | 2NT |
| pass | 3NT | all pass | |

Opening lead: ♠K

Declarer has to assume that West was dealt the ♡K. If East holds the ♡K the endplay will fail since West can exit with a heart. If West keeps the ♡K8, declarer must retain the ♡Q5 in dummy.

**North**
♠ 8 7 4
♡ 5 4
♢ A K 7 6 5 3
♣ 5 3

**West**
♠ Q J 10 6 5
♡ Q 9
♢ Q 10 2
♣ 9 8 6

*Dealer E
Both Vul.*

**East**
♠ 9 2
♡ J 10 8 7 6
♢ 9 8
♣ Q J 10 7

**South**
♠ A K 3
♡ A K 3 2
♢ J 4
♣ A K 4 2

| West | North | East | South |
|------|-------|------|-------|
|      |       | pass | 2NT   |
| pass | 3NT   | all pass |   |

Opening lead: ♠Q

When the ♢J is played and West plays the queen, declarer must duck in dummy and lose that trick.

**North**
♠ Q J 9 4
♡ A J 10 8 5
♢ 6 2
♣ A 4

**West**
♠ 7 3
♡ 9 7
♢ K Q 9 7 5
♣ K 9 8 2

*Dealer W
Neither Vul.*

**East**
♠ 6 5 2
♡ 6 3
♢ A J 10
♣ Q J 10 6 3

**South**
♠ A K 10 8
♡ K Q 4 2
♢ 8 4 3
♣ 7 5

| West | North | East | South |
|------|-------|------|-------|
| pass | 1♡    | pass | 1♠    |
| pass | 2♠    | pass | 4♡    |
| pass | 4♠    | all pass |   |

Opening lead: ♢K

In a spade contract declarer can win eleven tricks but in the nine-card heart fit only ten tricks.

## PROBLEM 19

**North**
- ♠ 8 6 2
- ♡ K 9 8
- ◇ J 7 6 4
- ♣ A Q 5

**West**
- ♠ Q J 10 9 7
- ♡ 7 6 4
- ◇ A 3
- ♣ 9 4 2

*Dealer W*
*Neither Vul.*

**East**
- ♠ 5 3
- ♡ Q J 3 2
- ◇ K 2
- ♣ J 10 8 6 3

**South**
- ♠ A K 4
- ♡ A 10 5
- ◇ Q 10 9 8 5
- ♣ K 7

| West | North | East | South |
|------|-------|------|-------|
| pass | pass | pass | 1NT |
| pass | 3NT | all pass | |

Opening lead: ♠Q

The spade card that is removed from the West hand must be placed in North's hand. It is essential that East still has only two spades. If East had three spades it would make no difference whether declarer held up on the first or second round.

## PROBLEM 20

**North**
- ♠ 8 7 6
- ♡ A 4
- ◇ A Q 10 4
- ♣ K 7 6 3

**West**
- ♠ Q 9 4
- ♡ K J 10 9 5
- ◇ 8 6 3
- ♣ A 4

*Dealer W*
*Both Vul.*

**East**
- ♠ 10 5 3 2
- ♡ 8 7 6 3
- ◇ 7 2
- ♣ Q J 2

**South**
- ♠ A K J
- ♡ Q 2
- ◇ K J 9 5
- ♣ 10 9 8 5

| West | North | East | South |
|------|-------|------|-------|
| pass | 1◇ | pass | 3NT |
| all pass | | | |

Opening lead: ♡J

North has only four diamonds so that declarer only has eight top tricks after the opening lead.

**North**
♠ K 4
♡ 8 6 3
◇ 9 8 7 4
♣ 8 7 5 2

**West**
♠ 8 7 5 3 2
♡ Q 9 7 4
◇ K J 10
♣ 9

*Dealer S*
*EW Vul.*

**East**
♠ 6
♡ A K J 10 5 2
◇ Q 6
♣ 10 6 4 3

**South**
♠ A Q J 10 9
♡ —
◇ A 5 3 2
♣ A K Q J

| West | North | East | South |
|------|-------|------|-------|
|      |       |      | 2♣    |
| pass | 2◇    | 2♡   | 2♠    |
| 4♡   | 4♠    | all pass | |

Opening lead: ♡4

Fear of a 5-1 trump split should provoke declarer to discard diamonds rather than ruffing a heart on the first three tricks. Even if the spade suit splits 3-3 or 4-2, declarer cannot make more than ten tricks.

**North**
♠ 5 4 2
♡ 10 8 5
◇ A K Q 2
♣ 6 5 2

**West**
♠ K 7 3
♡ 6 4 3
◇ J 10 9 8
♣ A K Q

*Dealer W*
*Neither Vul.*

**East**
♠ 10 9 8 6
♡ 9 2
◇ 7 6 4
♣ J 10 8 3

**South**
♠ A Q J
♡ A K Q J 7
◇ 5 3
♣ 9 7 4

| West | North | East | South |
|------|-------|------|-------|
| 1◇   | pass  | pass | 2♡    |
| pass | 3♡    | pass | 4♡    |
| all pass | | | |

Opening lead: ♣A

West takes three club tricks and shifts to the ◇J. If declarer runs five heart winners, West is squeezed.

## PROBLEM 23

**North**
♠ A Q 9
♡ J 10 8 2
♢ 7 4 3
♣ A J 9

**West**
♠ 7 6 3
♡ 7 6 5 3
♢ K J 5
♣ 4 3 2

*Dealer E*
*EW Vul.*

**East**
♠ 8
♡ A K Q 9 4
♢ A Q 6 2
♣ 7 6 5

**South**
♠ K J 10 5 4 2
♡ —
♢ 10 9 8
♣ K Q 10 8

| West | North | East | South |
|------|-------|------|-------|
|      |       | 1♡   | 1♠    |
| 2♡   | 3♡    | 4♡   | 4♠    |
| pass | pass  | 5♡   | 5♠    |
| all pass |   |      |       |

Opening lead: ♡3

On this hand the dummy reversal is necessary to make the contract. Declarer must go to dummy twice in spades and twice in clubs. In order to profit from a dummy reversal with a 6-3 trump fit, declarer must ruff at least four cards in the long trump hand.

## PROBLEM 24

**North**
♠ Q J 10 6 5
♡ K Q J 10 5
♢ —
♣ Q J 10

**West**
♠ —
♡ A 9 8 3 2
♢ Q 9 4 2
♣ 9 8 7 4

*Dealer S*
*EW Vul.*

**East**
♠ 3 2
♡ 7 6 4
♢ A K J 10 7
♣ 6 5 2

**South**
♠ A K 9 8 7 4
♡ —
♢ 8 6 5 3
♣ A K 3

| West | North | East | South |
|------|-------|------|-------|
|      |       |      | 1♠    |
| pass | 4♢    | dbl  | 4♡    |
| pass | 4♠    | pass | 5♣    |
| pass | 5♢    | pass | 7♠    |
| all pass |   |      |       |

Opening lead: ♢2

Since declarer only needs four diamond ruffs, he should play one round of trumps. If spades are not 1-1, declarer must start ruffing diamonds.

# PROBLEM 25

**North**
♠ K 6
♡ A 5
◇ A 10 8 6
♣ A J 10 7 5

**West**
♠ J 9 8 2
♡ Q J 10 7
◇ Q J 4 2
♣ 6

*Dealer E*
*NS Vul.*

**East**
♠ Q 10 7 4
♡ 9 8 4 3
◇ 3
♣ 8 4 3 2

**South**
♠ A 5 3
♡ K 6 2
◇ K 9 7 5
♣ K Q 9

| West | North | East | South |
|------|-------|------|-------|
|      |       | pass | 1NT   |
| pass | 6NT   | all pass |   |

Opening lead: ♡Q

Declarer needs the extra club winner since the diamond suit can only produce three winners.

# PROBLEM 26

**North**
♠ Q 10 3
♡ 7 2
◇ Q J 9 5
♣ A Q 10 5

**West**
♠ 9 4 2
♡ K 6 3
◇ 8 6 4
♣ K J 9 4

*Dealer W*
*Both Vul.*

**East**
♠ 7 6 5
♡ A Q 9 8 4
◇ 10 7 3 2
♣ 3

**South**
♠ A K J 8
♡ J 10 5
◇ A K
♣ 8 7 6 2

| West | North | East | South |
|------|-------|------|-------|
| pass | pass  | pass | 1NT   |
| pass | 3NT   | all pass |   |

Opening lead: ♣4

Declarer knows that East does not have a club higher than dummy's ♣5

## PROBLEM 27

**North**
- ♠ 10 9 8 7 3
- ♡ Q 3
- ◇ A K 6 2
- ♣ K 4

**West**
- ♠ —
- ♡ J 8 7 2
- ◇ Q J 10
- ♣ J 9 8 7 5 2

*Dealer W*
*EW Vul.*

**East**
- ♠ 6
- ♡ A K 10 9 6 4
- ◇ 9 8 7
- ♣ A Q 3

**South**
- ♠ A K Q J 5 4 2
- ♡ 5
- ◇ 5 4 3
- ♣ 10 6

| West | North | East | South |
|------|-------|------|-------|
| pass | pass | 1♡ | 1♠ |
| 2♡ | 3♡[1] | 4♡ | 4♠ |
| all pass | | | |

1. Spade support and 10 or more points.

Opening lead: ♡2

Declarer must discard a diamond from South on the second round of hearts. There is only one discard provided by the diamond suit, but it is enough to avoid a loser since South started with only two clubs.

## PROBLEM 28

**North**
- ♠ A 6
- ♡ Q J 7 4 3
- ◇ K 7 5
- ♣ K Q 8

**West**
- ♠ 5
- ♡ 9 8
- ◇ A Q 9 4 3 2
- ♣ J 7 6 4

*Dealer E*
*Neither Vul.*

**East**
- ♠ J 8 4 2
- ♡ 10 6 2
- ◇ J 10 6
- ♣ 9 5 3

**South**
- ♠ K Q 10 9 7 3
- ♡ A K 5
- ◇ 8
- ♣ A 10 2

| West | North | East | South |
|------|-------|------|-------|
| | | pass | 1♠ |
| pass | 2NT | pass | 4♣ |
| pass | 4♡ | pass | 6♠ |
| all pass | | | |

Opening lead: ◇A, followed by the ◇Q

Even though declarer can win the second diamond trick with the king, he must resist that temptation and ruff in hand. It is necessary to ruff both the ◇K and a small diamond in order to shorten his trump suit.

**North**
♠ 7 6 3
♡ A K 3
◇ J 4 3
♣ A 7 6 3

**West**
♠ Q J 10 9 8 2
♡ 9 7
◇ A 6
♣ 10 5 2

*Dealer E*
*Both Vul.*

**East**
♠ 5 4
♡ Q J 10 5
◇ K 7 2
♣ Q J 9 8

**South**
♠ A K
♡ 8 6 4 2
◇ Q 10 9 8 5
♣ K 4

| West | North | East | South |
|------|-------|------|-------|
|      |       | pass | 1◇ |
| 1♠ | 2♠[1] | pass | 2NT |
| pass | 3NT | all pass | |

1. Asks for spade stopper.

Opening lead: ♠Q

Declarer cannot sever communications if spades break 5-3. Therefore he should pray that they break 6-2 and play accordingly.

**North**
♠ J 9 8 5
♡ 8
◇ Q 10 9 8 5 2
♣ A K

**West**
♠ Q 4 3
♡ 10 6 5 3 2
◇ A 6
♣ 9 8 7

*Dealer E*
*Neither Vul.*

**East**
♠ A K 6 2
♡ J 9 7 4
◇ K 4 3
♣ 6 3

**South**
♠ 10 7
♡ A K Q
◇ J 7
♣ Q J 10 5 4 2

| West | North | East | South |
|------|-------|------|-------|
|      |       | pass | 1♣ |
| pass | 1◇ | pass | 1NT |
| pass | 2NT | pass | 3NT |
| all pass | | | |

Opening lead: ♡3

Declarer only has to discard the ace and king of clubs to unblock the club suit.

**North**
♠ 9 6 4
♡ K Q J
◇ K Q J
♣ A 7 6 4

**West**
♠ A
♡ A 10 9 6 2
◇ A 5 2
♣ 10 9 5 2

Dealer W
Both Vul.

**East**
♠ Q J
♡ 8 7 4
◇ 10 8 7 4 3
♣ J 8 3

**South**
♠ K 10 8 7 5 3 2
♡ 5 3
◇ 9 6
♣ K Q

| West | North | East | South |
|------|-------|------|-------|
| 1♡ | 1NT | pass | 4♠ |
| all pass | | | |

Opening lead: ♣10

Since West almost
certainly holds the ♠A,
hope it is a singleton
and lead a low spade
from hand. Even if West
opened without the ♠A,
he will probably have both
the queen and jack. This
would leave East with a
singleton ace and declarer
will still succeed.

**North**
♠ Q 8 6 4 2
♡ 10 6 4
◇ A Q 10
♣ 6 4

**West**
♠ J
♡ A K Q J
◇ 9 6 4 3
♣ Q J 10 2

Dealer N
Both Vul.

**East**
♠ 10 7
♡ 9 8 3 2
◇ K J 5
♣ 9 8 7 3

**South**
♠ A K 9 5 3
♡ 7 5
◇ 8 7 2
♣ A K 5

| West | North | East | South |
|------|-------|------|-------|
| | pass | pass | 1♠ |
| dbl | 4♠ | all pass | |

Opening lead: ♡A

After stripping the hand,
declarer can play either
the ten or the queen
on the first round of
diamonds in order to
execute the endplay. The
ten is clearly the correct
play since if West has both
the king and jack, declarer
will have no diamond
losers.

## PROBLEM 33

**North**
- ♠ A K Q
- ♡ 7 6 5
- ◇ 8 4 3
- ♣ Q J 6 2

**West**
- ♠ 9 6 5
- ♡ J 10 9
- ◇ Q J 9 7
- ♣ A K 7

*Dealer E
Both Vul.*

**East**
- ♠ J 10 4 2
- ♡ K 8
- ◇ 10 5
- ♣ 10 9 8 4 3

**South**
- ♠ 8 7 3
- ♡ A Q 4 3 2
- ◇ A K 6 2
- ♣ 5

| West | North | East | South |
|------|-------|------|-------|
|      |       | pass | 1♡ |
| pass | 2♣ | pass | 2◇ |
| pass | 4♡ | all pass | |

Opening lead: ♣A, followed by the ◇Q

Three spade winners are needed in North in order to provide dummy with three entries. Declarer must be able to enter North once to take a heart finesse and twice more in order to lead both club honors.

## PROBLEM 34

**North**
- ♠ 7 4 2
- ♡ A K
- ◇ A K Q 5
- ♣ A 8 4 2

**West**
- ♠ Q J 10 9 6 3
- ♡ 8 6 2
- ◇ 10 8
- ♣ 7 6

*Dealer E
Both Vul.*

**East**
- ♠ 8 5
- ♡ J 10 7 4
- ◇ 9 7 3
- ♣ J 10 9 5

**South**
- ♠ A K
- ♡ Q 9 5 3
- ◇ J 6 4 2
- ♣ K Q 3

| West | North | East | South |
|------|-------|------|-------|
|      |       | pass | 1NT |
| pass | 4♣[1] | pass | 4♡ |
| pass | 7NT | all pass | |

1. Gerber.

Opening lead: ♠Q

The ♣3 provides South with the necessary communication for a simple squeeze. When declarer plays two top spades and four top diamonds, East will be unable to keep both four clubs and four hearts.

## PROBLEM 35

**North**
♠ Q J
♡ A K J 10
♢ 8 6
♣ A 7 6 3 2

**West**
♠ 7 5
♡ 9 8 5 3 2
♢ 7 4
♣ K J 10 5

*Dealer W*
*Both Vul.*

**East**
♠ 10 9 8 2
♡ Q 7 4
♢ K Q J 10
♣ Q 9

**South**
♠ A K 6 4 3
♡ 6
♢ A 9 5 3 2
♣ 8 4

| West | North | East | South |
|------|-------|------|-------|
| pass | 1♣ | pass | 1♠ |
| pass | 2♣ | pass | 2♢ |
| pass | 2♡ | pass | 2NT |
| pass | 3NT | all pass | |

Opening lead: ♡3

Must resist the finesse. After winning the first heart trick and cashing the top spades in dummy, declarer should win a second heart trick and surrender a heart.

## PROBLEM 36

**North**
♠ K 5 2
♡ J 8 6 5 2
♢ K Q 5
♣ J 8

**West**
♠ 10 9 7
♡ A 9
♢ J 8 7 4
♣ 9 7 3 2

*Dealer W*
*Both Vul.*

**East**
♠ A 8 6 4
♡ 7
♢ 10 9 6 3 2
♣ A K 5

**South**
♠ Q J 3
♡ K Q 10 4 3
♢ A
♣ Q 10 6 4

| West | North | East | South |
|------|-------|------|-------|
| pass | pass | 1♢ | 1♡ |
| pass | 2♢[1] | pass | 4♡ |
| all pass | | | |

1. Heart support and 10 or more points.

Opening lead: ♡A

Since West led the ♡A, East must have the ♠A for his 1♢ bid. The only hope for declarer is to win the second heart in dummy and play a low spade off dummy. It probably won't work since East can cash two top clubs, but it is the only shot.

**North**
- ♠ K 6
- ♡ A J 10 8
- ◇ A 4 3
- ♣ K Q 5 2

| West | North | East | South |
|------|-------|------|-------|
|      |       | 1◇ | 1♡ |
| pass | 4NT | pass | 5♠[1] |
| pass | 6♡ | all pass | |

1. Two keycards and the trump queen.

Opening lead: ◇9

**West**
- ♠ 10 9 7 5 4
- ♡ 5
- ◇ 9 6
- ♣ 10 7 6 4 3

*Dealer E
Both Vul.*

**East**
- ♠ Q J 8
- ♡ 7
- ◇ K Q J 10 8
- ♣ A J 9 8

**South**
- ♠ A 3 2
- ♡ K Q 9 6 4 3 2
- ◇ 7 5 2
- ♣ —

Without the diamond lead, declarer would have a loser-on-loser play. That would succeed wherever the ♣A is located. The diamond lead, unfortunately, converted the two slow losers to fast losers, so declarer needs a successful ruffing finesse in order to avoid one of the diamond losers. Since East opened the bidding, it is almost certain to work.

**North**
- ♠ 9 8
- ♡ 8 7 4
- ◇ 7 5 3
- ♣ A K J 5 3

| West | North | East | South |
|------|-------|------|-------|
| pass | pass | pass | 2♣ |
| pass | 3♣ | pass | 6♠ |
| all pass | | | |

**West**
- ♠ 7 6
- ♡ 10 6 5 2
- ◇ 10 9 8 6
- ♣ Q 10 7

*Dealer W
Neither Vul.*

**East**
- ♠ 10 2
- ♡ K Q J
- ◇ J 4 2
- ♣ 9 8 6 4 2

Opening lead: ◇10

**South**
- ♠ A K Q J 5 4 3
- ♡ A 9 3
- ◇ A K Q
- ♣ —

The contract will be successful no matter which defender has the ♠10. Discarding the heart losers on the clubs will be very enjoyable.

# APPENDIX 1
## Everything You Ever Wanted to Know About Probability

# Why bother to read Appendix 1?

The goal of this appendix is to provide you with the basics of probability and show how probability can aid decision-making at the bridge table. The appendix explains the mathematics behind the play of several suit combinations. The approach does not assume that you have any prior experience in computing probabilities.

By the time you finish, you will understand when it is correct to base a decision on the table values that appeared in the *Introduction* on page 14 and when to ignore the tables. The best known maxim that bridge players use for deciding between a finesse against a queen or playing for a drop is *eight ever, nine never*. This appendix will provide you with the mathematical background to understand why this maxim causes me to cringe.

This appendix adds a certain completeness to the book. More than half of the problems include a statement about the probability of a event occurring without providing information as to how those values were obtained. At the end of this appendix, I refer back to all of those problems and justify my values.

*Appendix 2: Much More Than You Ever Wanted to Know About Probability* covers combinatorics and how the values in the tables were computed. After Appendix 2 there is a list of books on the mathematics of bridge.

DISCLAIMER: Throughout both appendices, I am rounding off values. Sometimes I am shading the truth very slightly in order to obtain values that are easier for bridge players either to remember or to understand. If you were a graduate student of mine in a probability course, *please*, no letters!

# Introduction to probability

The probability of an event is a numerical value that indicates how likely it is that the particular event will actually occur.

An essential tool in obtaining probabilities is to use the following formula:

$$P(\text{event } E) = \frac{\text{number of outcomes in which event E occurs}}{\text{number of all possible outcomes}}$$

This formula can only be applied when all possible outcomes are equally likely to occur. We will see many situations where this condition is not satisfied and a bridge player can easily be misled by trying to apply the formula.

The only possible numerical values for P(E) are greater than or equal to zero and less than or equal to one. That is described with mathematical notation as $0 \leq P(E) \leq 1$.

Examples: Pick a card from a shuffled bridge deck.

The probability that the card will be an ace is P(ace) = $\frac{4}{52}$ = $\frac{1}{13}$.

The probability that it will be a heart is P(heart) = $\frac{13}{52}$ = $\frac{1}{4}$.

The probability that it is a red ace is P(red ace) = $\frac{2}{52}$ = $\frac{1}{26}$.

The probability that it is a black card is P(black card) = $\frac{26}{52}$ = $\frac{1}{2}$.

The probability that it is an honor card is P(honor card) = $\frac{20}{52}$ = $\frac{5}{13}$.
(Honor cards include the 10.)

The probability that it is either a heart or a black card is
P(heart or black card) = $\frac{39}{52}$ = $\frac{3}{4}$.

The probability that it is either a heart or an honor card is
P(heart or honor card) = $\frac{28}{52}$ = $\frac{7}{13}$.

The probability that you will be the declarer on the next deal is
P(declarer) = $\frac{1}{4}$.

This is only correct if we assume that all four players are equally likely to be the declarer. If any of the players is a very timid or aggressive bidder this figure would be off.

How often would you expect to be the declarer in a 24-board session?

$\frac{1}{4}$ x 24 = 6

How often would you expect to be the declarer if you played 300 deals?

$$\frac{1}{4} \times 300 = 75$$

If you could keep a record of several hundred deals (one week of bridge for those living the good life) with your favorite partner, you may be able to demonstrate that he is a hand hog.

## Percentages and odds

In my bridge columns, I never use the term 'probability' but instead state a percentage to indicate how likely it is that an event will occur. I feel that it is easier for those bridge players who lack experience with probabilities to relate to percentages than to the more mathematical concept of probability.

Gamblers find it more convenient to think in terms of odds rather than either probabilities or percentages. The odds are useful for indicating the payoff for a bet of any size.

For example, if $P(E) = \frac{3}{5}$ when using probabilities, the chance of event E occurring expressed as a percentage is 60%, and the odds of that event occurring are 3 to 2. In a fair game (one which favors neither you nor your opponent), if you believe the probability that E will occur is $\frac{3}{5}$ and you place a bet that E will occur you should risk 3 dollars for a payoff of 2. Likewise, you should risk 30 dollars for a payoff of 20, and risk 60 for a payoff of 40. You can see how useful odds are for gamblers. Throughout both appendices, I will usually refer to probabilities rather than percentages or odds. On rare occasions, percentages or odds will be used.

## Adding probabilities

When two events cannot both occur at the same time they are called *mutually exclusive events*. In order to obtain the probability of either of those events occurring one can simply add together the probabilities of the two individual events.

**Example:** Suppose we are again drawing one card from a shuffled deck. In order to obtain the probability of either a heart or a black card, their respective probabilities can be added since they are mutually exclusive events. There are no cards that are both a heart and black.

Since we found that P(heart) = $\frac{1}{4}$ and P(black card) = $\frac{1}{2}$,

P(heart or black card) = P(heart) + P(black card) = $\frac{1}{4} + \frac{1}{2} = \frac{3}{4}$.

This result is the same value as obtained previously when we considered that 39 of the 52 cards are either a heart or black.

**Example:** In order to obtain the probability of a heart or an honor card we cannot simply add their respective probabilities. These two events are *not* mutually exclusive. There are five heart honor cards. These five cards would be counted twice. We must subtract the probability of getting one of those five cards.

Since we found that P(heart) = $\frac{1}{4}$, P(honor card) = $\frac{5}{13}$, and

P(heart honor card) = $\frac{5}{52}$,

P(heart or honor card) = $\frac{1}{4} + \frac{5}{13} - \frac{5}{52} = \frac{13}{52} + \frac{20}{52} - \frac{5}{52} = \frac{28}{52} = \frac{7}{13}$.

This result is the same value as obtained previously when we considered that 28 of the 52 cards are either a heart or an honor.

Throughout the Appendices, we will usually be dealing with mutually exclusive events. In these cases, we will simply be able to add their respective probabilities. The next example shows a common application.

**Example:** Suppose declarer is in an eight-card trump fit and he chooses a line of play that will succeed whenever the trump suit splits 3-2 or 4-1. What is the probability of success?

P(3-2 split) = 0.68   from a table in the *Introduction*.

P(4-1 split) = 0.28   from a table in the *Introduction*.

Since a suit cannot split both ways, these are mutually exclusive events.

Therefore, P(success) = 0.68 + 0.28 = 0.96

# Multiplying probabilities

We can often multiply probabilities to compute the probability of two events both occurring. One must realize that the occurrence of one event may affect the probability that the second event will occur.

**Example:** We previously found that if you chose one card from a deck, $P(ace) = \frac{4}{52}$.

If you select two cards from the deck, the probability that they are both aces **cannot** be obtained by multiplying $\frac{4}{52} \times \frac{4}{52}$. In order for both cards to be aces, the first card chosen must be an ace, so when the second is chosen, there are only 51 cards left and only three of them are aces.

Therefore, $P(\text{both aces}) = \frac{4}{52} \times \frac{3}{51} = 0.0045$.

**Example:** You are declarer (South) and dummy (North) has just hit the table. Ignore the opening lead. You are missing the ♠K. What is the probability that West has the king?

There are 26 missing cards held by the defenders, and West has 13 of them. The king can be any of those 26 cards.

$P(\text{West was dealt spade king}) = \frac{13}{26} = \frac{1}{2}$

This is often called the *vacant places principle*.

It is tempting to believe that if you observe the opening lead, this value would change since West would only have 12 missing cards. Actually this reasoning, which seems logical, is incorrect because the opening lead is not chosen at random. Suppose the defense holds no spade honors except the king. The ♠K would almost never be led. Therefore, when the ♠K is not led, you have not learned anything and should realize that the probability that West was dealt the king is still $= \frac{1}{2}$.

**Example:** What is the probability that West was dealt both the spade king and heart king?

$P(\text{West has spade and heart kings}) = \frac{13}{26} \times \frac{12}{25} = 0.24$

The $\frac{12}{25}$ results from the vacant places principle. If West holds the ♠K, he has only 12 vacant places out of the remaining 25 to hold the heart king. At the bridge table, declarer should simplify this calculation by treating this as $\frac{1}{2} \times \frac{1}{2} = \frac{1}{4}$.

If you have to finesse West for both kings, your chance that both finesses will be successful is approximately $\frac{1}{4}$.

**Example**: Declarer has an eight-card trump fit. The only honor that the defense holds in that suit is the queen. What is the probability of either defender holding queen doubleton?

This can only happen when the suit splits 3-2. P(3-2 split) = 0.68 from a table in the *Introduction*. In addition to this split occurring, the queen must be in the two-card suit rather than the three-card suit. P(queen in the two card suit) $= \frac{2}{5}$. It must be in two of the five vacant places in the suit.

P(3-2 split with queen doubleton) = 0.68 x $\frac{2}{5}$ = 0.27

**Example:** Same as last example except with specifically West holding queen doubleton.

P(3-2 split with West holding queen doubleton) = 0.68 x $\frac{2}{5}$ x $\frac{1}{2}$

= 0.135

**Example:** In a suit, declarer (South) has the 4 while dummy holds AKJ532. What is the probability of declarer's winning six tricks?

The only line of play that can succeed is to finesse the queen. This will only win six tricks when both the suit splits 3-3 and West holds the queen.

P(3-3 split) = 0.36 from a table in the *Introduction*.

P(West holds the queen) = $\frac{3}{6}$ = $\frac{1}{2}$.

Therefore, P(3-3 split with West holding the queen) = 0.36 x $\frac{1}{2}$ = 0.18

## Combining chances

Suppose, in order to prevail in a contract, declarer needs two finesses both to be successful. Those two finesses may be in the same suit, such as AQ10 opposite xxx, or in two different suits. Declarer may be finessing through the same defender twice or each defender once. If declarer has no other information about the lie of the cards, the probability of both plays succeeding is approximately $\frac{1}{2} \times \frac{1}{2} = \frac{1}{4}$. I used the word 'approximately', since as we saw in the last section, with the example of West being dealt both the ♠K and ♡K, if a defender holds one of those honors the vacant places principle indicates that the chances drop slightly that he also holds the other honor. For practical purposes at the bridge table, using the approximation of $\frac{1}{4}$ is fine. In similar cases, I will drop the word approximate.

**Example:** In order to prevail in a contract, declarer needs three finesses all to succeed.

P(three successful finesses) = $\frac{1}{2} \times \frac{1}{2} \times \frac{1}{2} = \frac{1}{8}$

**Example:** In order to make a contract, declarer needs at least one out of two finesses to succeed.

P(at least one out of two finesses succeed) = $\frac{1}{2} + \frac{1}{2} - \frac{1}{4} = \frac{3}{4}$

I hope you are not surprised by the subtraction of $\frac{1}{4}$. Since the two finesses are *not* mutually exclusive events, we cannot simply add their probabilities. The probability that both will succeed is $\frac{1}{4}$. Therefore, we must subtract that value, so that we don't count it twice.

In Problem 20, the success of a contract depended on one out of two finesses winning. In that problem it was necessary to take them in the proper order to give declarer both chances.

**Example:** In order to make a contract, declarer will need both a finesse to succeed and a suit to split 3-2. It may be the same suit or two different suits.

P(finesse *and* 3-2 split) = $\frac{1}{2} \times 0.68 = 0.34$

**Example:** In order to make a contract, declarer will need either a finesse to succeed or a suit to split 3-2. It may be the same suit or two different suits.

P(finesse *or* 3-2 split) = $\frac{1}{2} + 0.68 - (\frac{1}{2} \times 0.68) = 0.84$

In this example, if you forgot to subtract 0.34 an alarm should go off in your brain since it would result in the probability of an event greater than 1. This can never happen.

**Example:** In order to prevail in a contract, declarer will need at least one out of three finesses to succeed.

These three events are not mutually exclusive. The prior technique used for two events that are not mutually exclusive cannot be extended to three events in an intuitive fashion.

The following alternative approach is easier:

$$P(\text{all three finesses fail}) = \frac{1}{2} \times \frac{1}{2} \times \frac{1}{2} = \frac{1}{8}$$

Since if they don't all fail, at least one must succeed,

$$P(\text{at least one finesse succeeds}) = 1 - \frac{1}{8} = \frac{7}{8}.$$

## Likelihood of particular hands

In this section we will be finding the probability of being dealt a hand that meets certain criteria.

When you pick up your 13 cards, there are 635,013,559,600 possible bridge hands. This number is only for one person's hand, not the total deal with all four hands. That would be a much, much, much larger number. These 635 billion hands are all equally likely to occur. This is a very large number but an important one for bridge players. Appendix 2 indicates how this value is obtained. If a player plays two sessions (54 boards) a day, everyday, in a year he will only play 54 x 365 = 19,710 hands. In 100 years at that rate, one would play fewer than 2 million hands. All 160,000 ACBL members, playing two sessions a day for the next 100 years will play a total of about 320 billion hands (80 billion deals). Ignoring the fact that many hands are repeated due to chance and duplicate pair movements, over the next one hundred years, all ACBL members combined could not come close to playing all possible hands. There are too many hands and not enough time to play them. Tell that to your non-bridge playing friends when they ask whether bridge gets repetitive or boring or they inquire why you play so much!

When playing in an event with hand records, bridge players often blame the computer for making interesting but tricky distributional hands. I find myself defending an innocent computer. It is easy to make up random hands but much harder for the computer to differentiate between interesting hands and boring hands. The beauty of bridge is that randomly generated hands are interesting and tricky. One reason the hands might seem abnormal is that shuffled hands tend not to be random unless they are shuffled many, many times. Poorly shuffled hands tend to be less distributional than randomly generated hands. This belief that the computer is trying to trick players can prompt poor decisions at the table. I have heard players say that they should not have taken the percentage play since the hand was computer generated. Maybe they should not have taken the percentage play for a good bridge reason, but not because they feel a nasty computer is mocking them.

**Example:** $P(\text{hand consisting of 13 hearts}) = \dfrac{1}{635,013,559,600}$

$P(\text{hand consisting of 13 cards in one suit}) = \dfrac{4}{635,013,559,600}$

$P(\text{hand containing 37 high card points}) = \dfrac{4}{635,013,559,600}$

Since 37 HCP requires all 4 aces, 4 kings, 4 queens, and any one of the 4 jacks

$P(\text{hand containing fewer than 37 HCP}) = 1 - \dfrac{4}{635,013,559,600}$

$= \dfrac{635,013,559,596}{635,013,559,600}$

**Example:** One can figure out how many of the 635 billion hands have exactly any particular number of high card points. It is a lengthy process where one computes how many hands can be formed with each assortment of picture cards that add up to a specific value. For example, to obtain the value for 24 HCP, one might first consider 4 aces, 2 kings, and 1 queen and figure out how many hands can be formed. The technique appears in Appendix 2. Then one might consider 4 aces, 2 kings and 2 jacks and figure out how many hands can be formed. Yes, it is a lot of work. I did not do it: the following results can be obtained from the *Official Encyclopedia of Bridge*.

355 million hands can be formed with exactly 24 high card points.

711 million hands can be formed with exactly 23 high card points.

1334 million hands can be formed with exactly 22 high card points

Since 355 + 711 + 1334 = 2400, there are 2 billion, 400 million hands with 22, 23 or 24 HCP.

Given the information that a hand will have either 22 or 23 or 24 high card points,

$$P(24 \text{ high card points}) = \frac{355}{2400} = 0.148$$

$$P(23 \text{ high card points}) = \frac{711}{2400} = 0.296$$

$$P(22 \text{ high card points}) = \frac{1334}{2400} = 0.556$$

It is interesting to notice that even though there are three possibilities (22, 23, and 24 points) their corresponding probabilities are not each $\frac{1}{3}$. It is easy to make the mistake of thinking these three possibilities are equally likely to occur. Based on these probabilities, one is much more likely to pick up a hand with 22 points than a hand with 23 or 24 points combined.

Obviously not all hands have the appropriate shape to open notrump, but the effect is roughly proportional and the above values are still correct. Suppose your partner's bid of 2NT shows 22-24 high card points. He is much more likely to have 22 points than 24 points. These probabilities were obtained under the assumption that you have not looked at your own hand. The greater the number of points in your own hand, the greater the probability will be that your partner has 22 points rather than 24.

This principle appeared in Problem 16.

**Example:** What are the odds of being dealt a yarborough?

A description and the history of the term 'yarborough' appeared in Problem 9. There are 32 cards in the deck that are the spot card 9 or lower. The probability of the first card dealt being a 9 or lower is $\frac{32}{52}$. The probability that the second card dealt is 9 or lower is $\frac{31}{51}$ since only 31 of the remaining 51 cards are 9 or lower because one has already been removed. For the third card the probability is $\frac{30}{50}$ since two have already been removed. After continuing for all 13 cards, one need only multiply these 13 values to obtain the probability of a yarborough.

$$P(\text{yarborough}) = \frac{32}{52} \times \frac{31}{51} \times \frac{30}{50} \times \frac{29}{49} \times \frac{28}{48} \times \frac{27}{47} \times \frac{26}{46} \times \frac{25}{45} \times \frac{24}{44} \times \frac{23}{43} \times \frac{22}{42} \times \frac{21}{41} \times \frac{20}{40}$$

$$= 0.000547$$

This value is approximately $\frac{1}{1828}$.

Therefore, the odds of being dealt a yarborough are 1 to 1827.

Appendix 2 will demonstrate a more elegant way to obtain the probability of a yarborough.

## Using and abusing the tables

The information provided by the tables is only accurate when declarer lacks any knowledge about how any of the other suits are splitting. This is rarely the case since any bidding by the defense or the opening lead usually reveals at least a smidgen of information. As mentioned in the *Introduction* on page 15, even if the defense passed throughout the bidding with approximately half the points, declarer can draw the inference that all of the suits are probably breaking more evenly than indicated by the tables.

The tables are more useful to help declarer decide how likely he is to be successful with a particular line of play than to guide him on how to play a suit.

**Example:** What is the chance of winning four tricks in this suit by playing the three top winners rather than finessing?

Dummy

A 10 4 2

Declarer

K Q 3

If the suit is played in this fashion, there are three different ways declarer will win four tricks.
1) When it splits 3-3.
2) When it splits 4-2 with a doubleton jack.
3) When it splits 5-1 with a singleton jack.
No two of these three possibilities can occur at the same time so the probability of each can be obtained separately and those three values can be added together.

1) P(3-3 split) = 0.36 from table

2) P(4-2 split, doubleton jack) = P(4-2 split) x P(doubleton jack)

$= 0.48 \times \frac{2}{6} = 0.16$

The jack can be in any of six positions but only two of them are in the doubleton.

3) P(5-1 split, singleton jack) = P(5-1 split) x P(singleton jack)

$$= 0.15 \times \frac{1}{6} = 0.02$$

The jack can be in any of six positions but only one of them is in the singleton.

P(winning four tricks by playing three top) = 0.36 + 0.16 + 0.02 = 0.54

Now let's consider how to play this suit. There is a choice whether to play for the jack to drop or to finesse. This decision will probably disappear if declarer procrastinates. Declarer should obviously first win two tricks with the king and queen. If either opponent shows out the decision will disappear. Either you have a marked finesse (if East shows out) or you will learn that you are limited to only three tricks in this suit (if West shows out).

After the first two tricks, if both defenders follow, it is clear that our original table for six missing cards has to be modified. The splits of 6-0 or 5-1 are no longer possible. The values on the top two lines for 3-3 or 4-2 increase proportionately. Their values of 36% and 48% change to approximately 43% and 57% respectively.

Back to the actual play of this suit: if the jack dropped on the first or second round, declarer has four winners. No decision. Suppose the jack has not appeared on the first two rounds. On the third round declarer leads the 3. If West shows out or drops the jack, again, declarer does not face a decision. However, if West plays a spot card, declarer finally does have to choose between playing for the drop or finessing. This will be referred to as the **point of decision.** There are only two possibilities: either West started with Jxxx and East with xx or West with xxx and East with Jxx. Prior to playing any cards in this suit, the chance of the first holding was 0.16 and the second holding was 0.18. Therefore, since they are mutually exclusive and add up to 0.34, 66% of the time declarer will not have to face this decision. Well, what if declarer does actually face this decision? The mathematician in my head would say that since both possibilities increase their likelihood proportionately, and since the second holding is slightly more likely than the first, go with the second. This is called the *percentage play*. However, the bridge player in my head is shouting, 'Ignore the mathematician, he is an idiot'. The bridge player is right. Declarer should delay playing any tricks in this suit until as late as possible. By that time, declarer may have a full count of the hand, or at least a partial count. In Problem 8, declarer faced this very decision with a full count. The bridge player in my head should make this decision while the mathematician should sit quietly in the corner. Victor Mollo, through his character the Hideous Hog, indicated his disdain for the overuse of mathematics at the bridge table. Here are two quotes: 'Odds and percentages ... they take the place of thinking, which is why they are so popular' and 'When I take a fifty-fifty chance, I expect it to come off eight or nine times out of ten'.[1]

It is interesting to note that in the actual play, if your intent is to play for the drop when the decision occurs, your chance of success is 61%. Why is there a discrepancy between this figure and the 54% we stated at the beginning of this example? Declarer's intent was to play for the drop and not finesse. Of course, if declarer has a marked finesse, he will take it. He is no fool. There is approximately an 8% chance that East will show out on the first or second round. Since we already counted the particular holding of West with xxxxx and East singleton jack, and we don't want to count it twice, there is a net increase of 7%. Therefore, the chance of winning four tricks is 0.54 + 0.07 = 0.61.

## Point of decision

This book has emphasized throughout the 38 Problems that the principle demonstrated by a hand has many more general applications than that specific deal. For that reason, I included the exercises where readers are asked to create their own deals that demonstrate the same principle. This obviously carries over to the play of a specific suit. It is important to consider both similar suits that should be played in the same manner and similar suits that declarer should play in a different way.

For all the examples assume that the other suits provide any necessary entries.

---

1. Mollo, Victor. *Bridge in the Menagerie.*

**Example:** Does the mathematical analysis for this suit differ from the last example?

Dummy
A K Q 10

Declarer
4 3 2

This suit is identical to the previous example. All of the analysis is still true.

**Example:** Does the mathematical analysis for this suit differ from the last example?

Dummy
A 4 3 2

Declarer
K Q 10

The probability of either the suit splitting 3-3 or dropping the jack is still 54% as in the previous two examples. The chance during actual play of winning four tricks, however, is slightly less than the previous examples. With this holding, declarer will have to decide whether he wants to finesse or not on the second round of this suit. Declarer can cash the king, enter dummy and lead low toward the Q-10. Since the point of decision is on the second round rather than the third, he will only have a marked finesse if West shows out on the first round. Declarer can still try to gain information by first playing other suits but is limited by the earlier point of decision when playing this suit. The probability of winning four tricks only increases by 1% to 55%. With the point of decision on the second round, the chance of success is reduced.

**Example:** Does the mathematical analysis of this suit differ from the last example?

Dummy
A K 3 2

Declarer
Q 10 4

This is identical to the last example where the point of decision was also on the second round.

**Example:** What is the chance of winning four tricks in this suit by playing the three top winners rather than finessing?

Dummy
A K Q 10

Declarer
3 2

Having only six cards in the suit substantially reduces declarer's prospects of dropping the jack.

P(4-3 split, jack third) = P(4-3 split) x P(jack third) = $0.62 \times \frac{3}{7} = 0.27$

P(5-2 split, jack doubleton) = P(5-2 split) x P(jack doubleton) $= 0.31 \times \frac{2}{7}$

$= 0.09$

P(6-1 split, jack singleton) = P(6-1 split) x P(jack singleton)

$= 0.07 \times \frac{1}{7} = 0.01$

These three potential opportunities to drop the jack total only 0.37. The chance that a defender shows out on the first round is less than 1%. Therefore, declarer should clearly finesse on the second round unless some strong bridge information indicates otherwise.

**Example:** What is the chance of winning five tricks in this suit by playing the two top winners rather than finessing?

North
A J 9 5

South
K 10 8 7 6

There are two ways to win five tricks, if the suit splits 2-2 or if it splits 3-1 with a singleton queen. Since these two events are mutually exclusive, their probabilities can be obtained separately and the two values can be added.

P(2-2 split) = 0.40

P(3-1 split, singleton queen) = P(3-1 split) x P(singleton queen)

$= 0.50 \times \frac{1}{4} = 0.125$

P(winning five tricks by playing the ace and king) = 0.40 + 0.125

= 0.525

Now we will consider the actual play. Suppose you start with the ace. If East shows out on the first round, you will unfortunately learn that you must lose to the queen. If West shows out, you have a marked finesse for the queen and will win five tricks. Obviously, declarer should consider the expected length of both defenders in this suit. If declarer has any reason to expect East to be longer than West, the ace should be cashed first, but if there is any reason to suspect West to be longer, cash the king first. It would be nice to delay playing this suit to get a partial or full count on the hand. Unfortunately nine-card suits, particularly in a major, tend to be the trump suit, so declarer will probably be forced to make a decision in this suit on the first couple of tricks.

Suppose both defenders play a low card on the first round of this suit. After winning that trick with the ace, lead a card from dummy and suppose East follows with a low card. Now you face the point of decision. There are only two possibilities: West started with Qx and East xx or West started with x and East Qxx. The mathematician in my head would say that the first possibility is slightly more likely than the second (originally 2%). You have seen every card in this suit except the queen. East has already played a card on this trick but West has not. Therefore, West is slightly more likely to hold the queen, since at the point of decision, West has one more card in his hand than East.

Of course the bridge player in my head would say, 'Hold on a minute. The probability of success for either line of play is extremely close. Is there any information from the defender's bids or play that would indicate how the other suits are breaking?' If there is some reason to believe that West is longer than East in another suit, it might be better to finesse. However, declarer must be very careful about using information obtained from an opening lead. At the end of Appendix 2, a potential pitfall will be described.

The chance of success if declarer lacks any useful information and sets out to play for the drop is 57.5 %. When the ace was played on the first round, declarer gained the 5% chance of West showing out, thereby enabling declarer to have a marked finesse. Of course, if East shows out, the situation is hopeless. Declarer will be frustrated by his decision not to play the king on the first round.

A well-known maxim to guide declarers is *eight ever, nine never.* It implies that with an eight-card fit, declarer should finesse against the queen. With a nine-card fit, however, declarer should play for the queen to drop. Since this example involves a nine-card fit the maxim should govern declarer's decision. We have seen, however, that declarer faced a very close decision. There is only a slight advantage in playing for the drop, and if declarer can draw some useful inference, he may realize that it is better to finesse. Therefore, the word *never* in the maxim is clearly not correct. *Never* should really be replaced by 'probably not, but a close decision'. Unfortunately, *eight ever, nine probably not, but a close decision* does not have the nice memorable ring of *eight ever, nine never.*

**Example:** Suppose the jack and king are switched in the previous example.

Dummy
A K 9 5

Declarer
J 10 8 7 6

Now there are only two options: playing for the drop or finessing West. Declarer can no longer finesse East. Assuming no information prior to playing this suit, declarer should play a top honor to see whether the queen drops or either defender shows out. The mathematics behind whether declarer should finesse or not is identical to the last example. It slightly favors not finessing. Remember *eight ever, nine probably not, but a close decision.*

The standard maxim correctly indicates that the percentage play is to finesse with an eight-card suit. For some suit combinations, declarer should finesse on the first round, for others, on the second.

**Example:** How should declarer play this suit to win six tricks?

Dummy

A K J 10 5 4

Declarer

3 2

Declarer should finesse on the first round so that a winning finesse can be repeated. This play is necessary when West holds Qxxx. The probability of that holding is 0.28 x 4/5 x $\frac{1}{2}$ = 0.11. Unfortunately, finessing on the first round will result in unnecessarily losing a trick when East holds queen singleton. The probability of that holding, however, is only 0.28 x 1/5 x $\frac{1}{2}$ = 0.03.

**Example:** How should declarer play this suit to win five tricks?

Dummy

A K J 10 5

Declarer

4 3 2

Declarer should first play a top card, in case East has a singleton queen. His three-card holding still gives him the luxury of being able to finesse twice: on the second and third rounds.

Sometimes the suit combination may require declarer to face a different type of problem when choosing between two lines of play. One line involves potentially no losers but may result in two losers, whereas the alternative line will always result in one loser. A sort of a double or nothing situation, like on a TV game show. You can take one loser, or go for none but risk two.

**Example:**

Dummy

A 9 8 5 2

Declarer

Q 10 7 6 3

If the ace is played on the first round, declarer will not lose any tricks in this suit if either defender holds the singleton king.

P(2-1 split, singleton king) = P(2-1 split) x P(singleton king)

$$= 0.78 \times \frac{1}{3} = 0.26$$

That is the good news. The bad news is that declarer will lose two tricks when West has the three missing cards. The probability of that is $0.22 \times \frac{1}{2} = 0.11$.

Even though declarer must make the crucial decision on the first round of this suit, the moment of decision can be slightly delayed by playing a low card toward the ace. If West plays the king, declarer plays the ace, losing no tricks in this suit. If West plays the jack, declarer should win the trick with the ace, and will now lose one trick, but no more than one, in this suit. If West shows out declarer can win the trick with the ace and play low to the queen, resulting in one loser. Only when West plays the missing spot card will declarer face a problem.

Declarer is at the point of decision. If he goes up with the ace, he will have no losers if East must play a singleton king, but he faces two losers, and an unwanted lesson on safety plays from his partner, if West was dealt all three missing cards. If, however, declarer plays the nine, he can never lose more than one trick. Even though declarer knows that West did not start with the singleton king, the chance that East holds a singleton king has risen from 13% to 26%. Since West holds the missing spot card, the chance that West has all three missing cards has risen from 11% to 22%. This close decision must be made by a bridge player and not a mathematician.

At any form of scoring other than matchpoint play, declarer should be guided by the requirements of making the contract. At matchpoint play, declarer may wish to jeopardize a cold contract for an overtrick. The decision often involves considering what contracts the rest of the field may be playing in and how successful declarer's play has been up to this point on this hand. For example, did the opening lead give declarer a trick or hurt him? In short, the mathematician should be viewed as no more than a consultant merely useful for providing a bridge player with information.

# Percentages in the Problems

Throughout the problems, I have often indicated the probability of an event. In this section, I will indicate the problem number, percentage, and how it was obtained.

## Problem 4

**33%**   THE EASY WAY:  Look in the *Official Encyclopedia of Bridge* for the table that provides the probability for a 4-4 split when 8 cards are held by the defense.  I did not include this table in the *Introduction* since it is less useful than the others.

THE HARD WAY: Use the same technique, for a 3-3 split, explained in Appendix 2 to obtain the probability for a 4-4 split.

$$P(\text{4-4 split}) = P(\text{West has four diamonds}) = \frac{8C4 \times 18C9}{26C13} = \frac{70 \times 48620}{10400600}$$
$$= 0.327$$

**62%**   This value appears in a table for a 4-3 split.

## Problem 6

**1%**   Value of 7% appears in a table for 6-1 split.

$P(\text{singleton is the queen}) = 1/7$

$P(\text{6-1 split, singleton queen}) = 0.07 \times \frac{1}{7} = 0.01$

**50%**   $\frac{13}{26}$ plus less than 1% for dropping the queen (1st round) and avoiding a losing finesse.

**9%**   Value of 31% appears in a table for 5-2 split.

$P(\text{doubleton contains the queen}) = \frac{2}{7}$

$P(\text{5-2 split, doubleton queen}) = 0.31 \times \frac{2}{7} = 0.09$

## Problem 9

**1827 to 1** Explained earlier in this Appendix.

**30%** Value of 50% appears in a table for a 3-1 split. Value of 10% appears in a table for a 4-0 split. Since mutually exclusive,

P(3-1 or 4-0 split) = 0.60 and P(East having 3 or 4 cards) = 0.30

**49%** Using the technique in Appendix 2,

P(East having 3 hearts) = $\frac{4C3 \times 8C2 \times 14C8}{8C2 \times 18C11}$ = 0.38

P(East having 4 hearts) = $\frac{4C4 \times 8C2 \times 14C7}{8C2 \times 18C11}$ = 0.11

P(East having 3 or 4 hearts) = 0.38 + 0.11 = 0.49

## Problem 11

**about 25%** P(West has the diamond queen) = $\frac{1}{2}$

P(East has the diamond 10 given that West has diamond queen) = $\frac{13}{25}$

P(East has diamond 10 and West has queen) = $\frac{1}{2} \times \frac{13}{25} = \frac{13}{50}$

**better than 60%** West is virtually certain to have the $\Diamond$Q and since West has all the missing aces and picture cards, he has only seven spot cards and is less likely than East to hold the $\Diamond$10.

## Problem 13

**36%** This value appears in a table for a 3-3 split.

## Problem 15

**27%** Value of 68% appears in a table for a 3-2 split.

P(doubleton contains the ace) = $\frac{2}{5}$

P(3-2 split, doubleton ace) = 0.68 x $\frac{2}{5}$ = 0.27

**13.5%** Since 27% is the probability that either defender holds ace doubleton, the probability for a specific defender is $\frac{1}{2}$ x 0.27 = 0.135

## Problem 16

**55% 30% 15%**  Explained earlier in this appendix.
**44% 33% 23%**  Same technique as for the 2NT range.
**60%**  $\quad$ P(East has the heart king) $= \dfrac{12}{20}$

## Problem 21

**36%**  This value appears in a table for a 3-3 split.
**48%**  This value appears in a table for a 4-2 split.
**84%**  Since mutually exclusive events, 0.36 + 0.48 = 0.84

## Problem 22

**50%**  East and West are equally likely to hold the spade king.
**Less than 25%**  $\quad$ P(West has four or more diamonds) = 0.50
Since West has more diamonds than East, he is slightly less likely than East to hold the ♠K.  P(West has the ♠K and four or more diamonds) is slightly less than 0.50 x 0.50 = 0.25

## Problem 24

**62%**  This value appears in a table for a 4-3 split.

## Problem 25

**68%**  This value appears in a table for a 3-2 split.
**11%**  The value 28% appears in a table for a 4-1 split. $\dfrac{2}{5}$ is the probability that the singleton is either the jack or queen. $0.28 \times \dfrac{2}{5} = 0.112$
**Almost 80%**  since these events are mutually exclusive 0.68 + 0.11 = 0.79

## Problem 28

**68%**  This value appears in a table for a 3-2 split.

## Problem 30

**68%**  This value appears in a table for a 3-2 split.

## Problem 31

**34%**  Value of 68% appears in a table for a 3-2 split.

P(East holds king) = $\frac{1}{2}$

P(East holding Kx or Kxx) = $0.68 \times \frac{1}{2} = 0.34$

## Problem 32

**approximately 75%**

P(East holds the diamond king) = $\frac{1}{2}$

P(East holds the diamond queen given he holds the king) = $\frac{12}{25}$

P(East holds both the diamond king and queen) = $\frac{1}{2} \times \frac{12}{25} = \frac{12}{50}$
= 0.24

P(East does not hold both the diamond king and queen)
= 1 − 0.24 = 0.76

## Problem 33

**68%**  This value appears in a table for a 3-2 split.
**36%**  This value appears in a table for a 3-3 split.
**48%**  This value appears in a table for a 4-2 split.
**84%**  Since mutually exclusive events 0.36 + 0.48 = 0.84

## Problem 35

**36%**  This value appears in a table for 3-3 split.

## Problem 37

**approximately 75%**

P(East holds the club queen) = 0.5

P(West holds the club ace given he does not hold the queen) = $\frac{13}{25}$

P(East holds the club queen, West holds the club ace) = $0.5 \times \frac{13}{25}$
= 0.26

P(East does not hold the club queen or West does not hold the club ace) = 1 − 0.26 = 0.74

## Problem 38

**0.214%** There are 635,013,559,600 total possible bridge hands. Of these 1,357 million have 23 or more points.

Therefore, $\dfrac{1,357,000,000}{635,000,000,000} = 0.00214$

**12%** Value of 50% appears in a table for 3-1 split.

P(singleton is the 10) = $\dfrac{1}{4}$

P(3-1 split, singleton 10) = $0.50 \times \dfrac{1}{4} = 0.125$

## Afterword

**Approximately 5%** Value of 31% appears in a table for a 5-2 split.

P(5-2 split, East has doubleton king) = $0.31 \times \dfrac{2}{7} \times \dfrac{1}{2} = 0.044$

Value of 7% appears in a table for a 6-1 split.

P(6-1 split, East has singleton king) = $0.07 \times \dfrac{1}{7} \times \dfrac{1}{2} = 0.005$

Since these two events are mutually exclusive,

P(East has doubleton or singleton king) = 0.044 + 0.005 = 0.049

---

# APPENDIX 2
## Much More Than You Ever Wanted to Know About Probability

# Why bother to read Appendix 2?

Any reader who survived Appendix 1 has acquired the mathematical background to read this second appendix. By the end of this appendix you will understand how the tables for various suit splits, shown on page 14 of the *Introduction,* are obtained. Most intermediate and advanced players have a working knowledge of those tables but are not aware of how their values are calculated. Reading this appendix will satisfy some bridge players' intellectual curiosity. Every year or so a bridge player asks me how the values in the tables were computed. I have an opportunity in this appendix to provide a clear answer to that question. Virtually all probabilities relating to suit distributions can be obtained by applying one powerful technique. Unfortunately this procedure requires more computation than a player can do at the bridge table.

Suppose declarer believes a suit is splitting 6-1 based on a weak two-bid made by a defender. Clearly, the values in the tables for the other three suits are no longer appropriate. The technique introduced in this appendix can still be used in the post-mortem to find the probabilities of the splits in the other suits. On the surface it might seem rather useless since the hand is finished before these calculations can be carried out. It appears only to help you defend your chosen line of play to your partner. I believe understanding the formula and applying it yourself will improve your intuition about suit splits. When you appreciate how a tool works, you are more comfortable using it and are more likely to use it correctly.

## Combinatorics

The term *combinatorics* refers to a branch of mathematics where one studies how many ways an event can occur. As we have seen, many probability problems can be solved by just obtaining the numerator and denominator of the fraction in the probability formula introduced at the beginning of Appendix 1. Sometimes obtaining them can be quite involved. A basic knowledge of combinatorics is needed, and in this section we'll develop the necessary tools.

If two activities are required for an event, the number of ways both activities can occur is obtained by multiplication. That is, if one activity can be performed in **m** ways and a second activity can be performed in **n** ways, the number of ways both can be done is **m** x **n**. This statement can be extended to more than two activities.

**Example:** At a Regional you plan to play on Friday and Saturday. On Friday you can play with any of 3 partners. On Saturday you can play with any of 5 partners. The total number of ways you can choose your partners for the two days is 3 x 5 = 15. Of course, after rejecting so many partners, you will have fewer options at the next Regional!

**Example:** Consider a poker hand consisting of five cards. How many different arrangements can be made with the five cards?

> Any arrangement of five cards can be viewed as a placement of a card in each of the five positions. Suppose the five cards are ♡2, ◇Q, ♠9, ♣J, and ◇3.

> Any of these five cards can be placed in the first position. Suppose the ♠9 is placed in the first position.

> Any of the remaining four cards can be placed in the second position. Suppose the ◇Q is placed there.

> Any of the remaining three cards can be placed in the third position. Suppose the ◇3 is placed there.

> Either of the remaining two cards can be placed in the fourth position. Suppose the ♣J is placed there.

> Only one card (the remaining ♡2) can be placed in the fifth position.

Each time a card is placed in a position an activity is performed. Therefore one is performing five activities. The total number of arrangements of these five cards is 5 x 4 x 3 x 2 x 1 = 120

Unfortunately, whatever order you put the cards in, it is still a crummy poker hand.

**Example:** Suppose you are playing bridge with a slow partner and to kill time while waiting for his bid, you randomly start rearranging your 13 cards. How many ways can the 13 cards be arranged?

This is the same as the Poker hand example. With the 13 cards it is

13 x 12 x 11 x 10 x 9 x 8 x 7 x 6 x 5 x 4 x 3 x 2 x 1

= 6,227,020,800

Rather than writing out this long expression it can be written in a compact form as 13!. This representation is called *factorial notation*. It is read as '13 factorial'. 13! is a surprisingly big number. If you form a new arrangement every second and work nonstop 24 hours a day, it will take 197 years to form all arrangements of those 13 cards. Seems unbelievable, but it is not a misprint.

**Example:** At a Regional, how many ways can 6 people form a line to buy an entry?

6! = 720

The study of the number of different ways objects can be arranged is not particularly important to bridge players but the factorial notation is necessary for the following very important formula.

The number of ways **r** objects can be chosen from **n** objects is

$$nCr = \frac{n!}{r!(n-r)!}$$

Occasionally you may encounter 0!. This cannot be obtained in the standard fashion.

By definition, 0! = 1.

**Example:** Six guests at your home want to play bridge. How many ways can four be chosen to play?

$$6C4 = \frac{6!}{4!(6-4)!} = \frac{6!}{4!2!} = 15$$

**Example:** You have seven cards. How many five-card poker hands can be formed?

$$7C5 = \frac{7!}{5!(7-5)!} = \frac{7!}{5!2!} = 21$$

**Example:** How many ways can you select 13 cards from a bridge deck?

$$52C13 = \frac{52!}{13!(52-13)!} = \frac{52!}{13!39!} = 635,013,559,600$$

This large value of 635 billion should look familiar to you. It was used in many examples in Appendix 1.

Don't be put off by mistakenly thinking that obtaining nCr involves a lengthy computation. A $15 scientific calculator will be capable of evaluating the function nCr. The letter C is used to indicate that one is obtaining the number of **c**ombinations that can be formed.

Now that we have the most important formula in combinatorics, we are capable of obtaining more involved probabilities.

**Example:** What is the probability of being dealt a yarborough?

There are 32 cards in the deck that are the spot card 9 or lower. From those 32 cards 32C13 bridge hands can be formed. Therefore,

$$P(\text{yarborough}) = \frac{32C13}{52C13} = \frac{347,373,600}{635,013,559,600} = 0.000547$$

This value is approximately $\frac{1}{1828}$.

This same example was done by a less elegant method in Appendix 1. At that time it was done without the use of the tool for obtaining the number of combinations.

**Example:** How many hands can be formed with exactly a seven-card heart suit?

Since there are 13C7 ways of being dealt 7 hearts from the 13 hearts, and 39C6 ways of being dealt 6 cards that are not hearts from the 39 cards that are not hearts, the total number of hands that can be formed with 7 hearts is 13C7 x 39C6 = 1716 x 3,262,623 = 5,598,661,068.

**Examples:** What is the probability of a hand containing a seven-card heart suit?

$$P(\text{hand containing a seven card heart suit}) = \frac{13C7 \times 39C6}{52C13}$$

$$= \frac{1716 \times 3262623}{635,013,559,600} = 0.0088$$

$$P(\text{hand containing a seven card suit}) = \frac{4 \times 13C7 \times 39C6}{52C13}$$

$$= 4 \times 0.0088 = 0.0352$$

**Example:** How many hands can be formed with three spades, five hearts, two diamonds, and three clubs? What is the probability of being dealt such a hand?

There are 13C3 ways to choose 3 spades from the 13, 13C5 ways to choose 5 hearts from 13, 13C2 ways to choose 2 diamonds, and 13C3 ways to choose 3 clubs. The number of hands is:

13C3 x 13C5 x 13C2 x 13C3 = 286 x 1287 x 78 x 286
= 8,211,173,256

Therefore, P(hand containing 3 spades, 5 hearts, 2 diamonds, 3 clubs)

$= \frac{8,211,173,256}{635,013,559,600} = 0.01293$

You may be surprised that the value is only slightly more than 1% since a 5-3-3-2 shape is quite common. It is important to realize that this is the probability of one specific distribution. If we want the probability of being dealt any hand with 5-3-3-2 shape, we must consider that any of the four suits can be the five-card suit, any of the remaining three suits can be the two-card suit, and the two remaining suits must both be three-card suits. Therefore we must multiply the previous answer by 4 x 3 = 12. Therefore,

P(5-3-3-2 shape) = 12 x 0.01293 = 0.155

This value of approximately 15% is quite reasonable. The most common shape is 4-4-3-2. You will encounter it on 21.5% of your hands. Surprisingly, the most balanced shape 4-3-3-3 (10.5%) is less common than the unbalanced shape 5-4-3-1 (12.9%).

**Example:** What is the probability of a hand containing exactly three aces and two kings?

There are 4C3 ways to choose 3 aces from the 4, 4C2 ways to choose 2 kings from the 4, and 44C8 ways to choose 8 cards that are neither an ace nor a king from the 44 such cards.

Therefore, P(exactly 3 aces and 2 kings) $= \frac{4C3 \times 4C2 \times 44C8}{52C13}$

$= \frac{4 \times 6 \times 177,232,627}{635,013,559,600} = 0.0067$

**Example:** You just picked up your hand and you hold five hearts. What is the probability that your partner has exactly three hearts?

You hold 5 of the 13 hearts in the deck and 8 of the 39 cards that are not hearts. Therefore, the other three players have a total of 8 cards that are hearts and 31 cards that are not hearts. The 31 is obtained by subtracting their number of hearts from their total number of cards, 39 - 8 = 31.

The number of ways that your partner can have three of the eight missing hearts is 8C3. The number of ways that your partner can hold ten cards that are not hearts from the remaining 31 cards that are not hearts is 31C10. Your partner can hold 8C3 x 31C10 different hands with exactly three hearts.

Since you have in your own hand 13 of the 52 cards, the total number of hands your partner can hold from the remaining 39 cards is 39C13.

$$\text{P(partner has three hearts)} = \frac{8C3 \times 31C10}{39C13} = \frac{56 \times 44,352,165}{8,122,425,444} = 0.306$$

Likewise,

$$\text{P(partner has four hearts)} = \frac{8C4 \times 31C9}{39C13} = \frac{70 \times 20,160,075}{8,122,425,444} = 0.174$$

## Obtaining the tables in the Introduction

Now we have the tools to figure out all the values in the tables that appeared in the *Introduction*.

**Example:** Suppose you are declarer (South) and dummy has just appeared. This means you know where 26 specific cards of the 52 are located. How many possible hands can West hold from the remaining 26 cards if you don't look at the lead?

$$26C13 = \frac{26!}{13!(26-13)!} = 10,400,600$$

**Example:** Dummy has just appeared. Suppose declarer and dummy have a total of seven spades. What is the number of ways West can have exactly two spades? Don't try to draw any inferences from the opening lead.

The number of ways West can have two of the six missing spades is

6C2. The number of ways West can have 11 cards that are not spades from the 20 missing cards in the other three suits is 20C11. Therefore, the total number of hands that West can hold with exactly two spades is 6C2 x 20C11. Earlier we found that the total number of hands that West could hold is 26C13 = 10,400,600.

Therefore, P(West has 2 spades) = $\frac{6C2 \times 20C11}{26C13}$ = $\frac{15 \times 167960}{10400600}$ = 0.242

Obviously, if we figured out P(East has two spades) the calculations would be the same and the value would be 0.242. Since a 4-2 split requires that either West has two spades or East has two spades,

P(4-2 spade split) = P(West has 2 spades) + P(East has 2 spades)

= 0.242 + 0.242 = 0.484.

This is the value that appears in the *Introduction* on page 14 in the table for a 4-2 split with 6 missing cards.

Likewise,

P(West has 1 spade) = $\frac{6C1 \times 20C12}{26C13}$ = $\frac{6 \times 125970}{10400600}$ = 0.073

P(5-1 spade split) = P(West has 1 spade) + P(East has 1 spade)

= 0.073 + 0.073 = 0.146

This can be rounded off to the value in the table for a 5-1 split.

Similarly,

P(West has no spades) = $\frac{6C0 \times 20C13}{26C13}$ = $\frac{1 \times 77520}{10400600}$ = 0.0075

P(6-0 spade split) = P(West has no spades) + P(East has no spades)

= 0.0075 + 0.0075 = 0.015

P(West has 3 spades) = $\frac{6C3 \times 20C10}{26C13}$ = $\frac{20 \times 184756}{10400600}$ = 0.355

The probability of East having three spades does not have to be computed since it only occurs when West has three spades. Therefore, P(3-3 spade split) = P(West has three spades) = 0.355

We have completed the whole table for missing six cards. These computed values are more accurate than the table values but are harder to remember. If you want to impress bridge players with this technique let them know that it is based on the hypergeometric distribution.

**Example:** Declarer and dummy have 8 spades. What is the probability of a 4-1 split in the defense?

$$P(\text{West has one spade}) = \frac{5C1 \times 21C12}{26C13} = \frac{5 \times 293930}{10400600} = 0.141$$

$$P(4\text{-}1 \text{ spade split}) = P(\text{West has 1 spade}) + P(\text{East has 1 spade})$$
$$= 0.141 + 0.141 = 0.282$$

This result agrees with the table value for a 4–1 split.

**Example:** Suppose West opened a weak two-bid in hearts. Declarer and dummy hold eight diamonds and six hearts. Since the defenders don't use a weak two-bid with a five-card suit, declarer can reasonably assume that hearts are breaking 6-1. What is the probability of a 4-1 diamond split?

The probability of West having one diamond and East four is not the same as East having one diamond and West four. Both values must be obtained.

$$P(4\text{-}1 \text{ split with West holding one diamond}) = \frac{5C1 \times 7C6 \times 14C6}{7C6 \times 19C7} = 0.298$$

5C1 is the number of ways to choose one diamond from the five missing diamonds.

7C6 is the number of ways to choose six hearts from the seven missing hearts.

14C6 is the number of ways to choose six cards that are neither hearts or diamonds.

19C7 is the number of ways to choose seven cards that are not hearts.

$$P(4\text{-}1 \text{ split with East holding one diamond}) = \frac{5C1 \times 7C1 \times 14C11}{7C1 \times 19C12} = 0.036$$

East would have to hold one diamond, one heart, and eleven cards that are neither hearts nor diamonds.

$$P(4\text{-}1 \text{ split}) = P(4\text{-}1 \text{ split with West holding one diamond})$$

$$+ P(4\text{-}1 \text{ split with East holding one diamond}) = 0.298 + 0.036 = 0.334$$

We see that the weak two-bid by West increased the likelihood of another suit breaking 4-1. The probability of East having four diamonds is eight times as great as that of West having four diamonds.

Consider the last two examples. It was necessary in this last example to change the suit from spades to diamonds since most bridge players consider it sacrilegious to open a weak two-bid with a four-card major in another suit. It would have been totally inappropriate to apply our mathematics when it violates a bridge principle.

One must be careful when trying to base decisions on certain biased information. For example, suppose declarer is in a notrump contract and the opening lead by West indicates that East started with a singleton and West with a seven-card suit. This extreme split would be clear evidence that West is more likely than East to be short in the other suits. Now suppose the opening lead indicates that West has four cards in the suit and East three. Remember, West will usually lead a long suit. West probably does not have a five-card suit. East is more likely than West to hold a five-card suit. Certainly, declarer should not get excited that he learned that West has one more card than East in the led suit. Declarer should expect the opening leader to usually lead a suit in which he has more cards than his partner.

Don't get lost in the mathematics. We play bridge, not mathematics!

---

# Further Readings on the Use of Probability in Bridge

Borel, Emile and André Chéron, *The Mathematical Theory of Bridge.* Transl. and ed. Alec Traub. Taiwan, n.d.

Francis, Henry, editor-in-chief, Dorthy Francis and Alan Truscott, *The Official Encyclopedia of Bridge*, 6th ed., Memphis, Tenn.: ACBL, 2001.

Goren, Charles, *Go with the Odds; A Guide to Successful Gambling*, London: The Macmillan Co., 1969.

Kelsey, Hugh and Michael Glauert, *Bridge Odds for Practical Players.* Master Bridge Series. London: Victor Gollancz and Peter Crawley, 1980.

Reese, Terence and Roger Trézel, *Master the Odds in Bridge*, New York: Frederick Fell, 1979.

Vivaldi, Antonio and Gianni Barracho, *Probabilities and Alternatives in Bridge.* Trans. and ed. Phil King. London: Batsford, 2001.

# Index of Types of Plays

If you enjoyed this book, be sure to pick up Julian Laderman's
2006 ABTA Book of the Year:

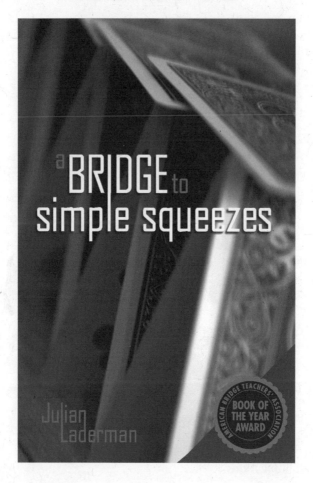